BENJAMIN BRITTEN'S OPERAS

Other works by Michael Wilcox

Plays: Volume One
Including: "Rents", "Accounts", "Lent", "Massage"
(Methuen Contemporary Dramatists 1997)

Outlaw in the Hills: A Writer's Year
(Methuen 1991)

Editor: *Gay Plays Vols 1–5*
(Methuen)

Outlines

BENJAMIN BRITTEN'S OPERAS

MICHAEL WILCOX

Absolute Press

First published in 1997 by Absolute Press
Scarborough House, 29 James Street West,
Bath, Somerset, England BA1 2BT
Tel: 01225 316013 Fax: 01225 445836
email sales@absolute press.demon.co.uk

Distributed in the United States of America and Canada by
Stewart, Tabori and Chang
115 West 18th Street, New York, NY 10011

Cover and text design by Ian Middleton

Cover printed by Devenish and Co. Bath
Printed by The Cromwell Press, Melksham

ISBN 1 899791 60 4

Contents

BENJAMIN BRITTEN AGED NINE YEARS, 1923

Introduction

There was a time in the early sixties when Benjamin Britten's music took my life by the scruff of the neck and wouldn't let go. Especially memorable were world premières of *A Midsummer Night's Dream* (1960), the *War Requiem* (1962), *Symphony for Cello and Orchestra* (1963) and *Curlew River* (1964). On each occasion, the BBC radio's Third Programme would be in faithful attendance, as it invariably was with Britten premières, and I would record the performance with my reel-to-reel tape recorder. Then there were crucial revivals of *Billy Budd* in its new two act version at Covent Garden, and the concert performance of *Gloriana*, Britten's much maligned Coronation opera, on the night of the Kennedy assassination, which started that great work's rehabilitation. I was able to attend both a dress rehearsal and two performances of *Billy Budd* and marvel at the beauty and clarity of Richard Lewis's peerless singing of Captain Vere. I scarcely had time to digest one memorable Britten performance when another followed fast on its heels. One week Britten would be playing Schubert and Mozart with Richter, then Britten would be conducting Rostropovich in Haydn. Later, at the end of the sixties there was *Peter Grimes* on television, with Peter Pears, soaked through and unhinged, making an unforgettable entry into 'The Boar' at the height of the storm to sing of ' . . . the Great Bear and Pleiades'. For some half-men half-boys, the sixties meant The Beatles, Woodstock, LSD, weed and magic mushrooms, but not to me. I felt alienated from most of my contemporaries as I queued for the galleries at Covent Garden and Sadler's Wells, searched the shops for the most affordable recording tape and begged or borrowed all available recordings of Britten's music, but I wasn't entirely alone, and looking back, I'm sure I had the best of it.

How curious that so many of the young British composers I know today hold Britten in something approaching contempt. On closer questioning, it is clear that they haven't actually listened to much Britten or studied his scores in detail. Instead, they have been influenced by the negative attitudes of their teachers and a shared assumption that Britten's music is dated and retrogressive and therefore not worth the time of day. Something of this surfaced again in 1996 when the local worthies of Aldeburgh refused to approve the erection of a statue of Britten in the town he made internationally famous. Especially regrettable were the remarks of Malcolm Williamson, Master of the Queen's Musick:

> 'A huge amount of literature is coming out now, since Ben's death. The homosexual, paedophilia thing is coming to the fore and there's going to be a terrific swing against him. That's nothing to me . . . he was a friend, although an ambidextrous friend . . . a backstabber, too. More and more facts are coming out about Britten and his dirty tricks . . . '

Anyone writing about Britten today has to step warily between what is left of the inner Britten circle, for whom Britten could do no wrong, and those who were wildly jealous of his success and damaged by first his acquaintance and then his sudden, irrational rejection.

The Britten–Pears partnership was also tantalizing. Could it really be possible that these two men were lovers, as I suspected? If this seems impossibly naïve from the perspective of the nineties, the fact that they were lovers came as a surprise even to those who knew them well. Susana Walton, in *William Walton: Behind the Facade* (OUP, 1988), describes her shock at realizing that Pears and Britten shared a double bed when they came to stay for the weekend. To my young and virginal sensibilities the thought that they might be queers was uncomfortable and grotesque. If I was as queer as I thought I might be, would I end up like that? How fervently I hoped not. And how could they possibly find each other attractive? I wasn't aware that I knew any homosexuals at the time, and the young men that dazzled me couldn't possibly be anything other than straight, could they? The fact that the whole subject was taboo and not to be talked about, even in the sixties, was both a relief and a frustration.

Anyway, I was sure there wasn't anyone I could talk to. So it seemed easier to shelve the problem and thrive on the music. There were settings of poems by Auden, Rimbaud, Michelangelo and, with *War Requiem*, by Wilfred Owen. All were homosexuals. In the operas, there were boys constantly under the threat of abuse, sexual or otherwise, something with which I could readily identify. Isaac awaited his father's sacrificial knife, the apprentice a bruising assault from Grimes, and Miles, a boy at boarding school returning to a huge house in the holidays just as I did, only to be torn apart by a hysterical governess and the seductive attentions of Peter Quint's ghost. All were part of my story, with my own father dying in the room next to mine when I was eight, and with his presence after death as strong in our household as it was in life. So much of Britten's music spoke directly to the boy in me, as though the composer was playing Quint, hinting at unmentionable desire and ravishing my young senses.

Thirty years and several lifetimes later, writing briefly about all the operas, and adopting an explicitly gay perspective, has proved fascinating and perplexing by turns. Britten's love of young boys, apparently more in the head than the bed if Humphrey Carpenter's absorbing biography of the composer is to be believed (Faber and Faber, 1992), is now a matter of public knowledge and casts the operas and the relationships of the characters within them in a fresh and revealing light. By contrast, the late Christopher Headington's biography of Peter Pears (Faber and Faber, 1992), although full of bald facts, fails to bring his subject to life at all, making the tenor seem so tedious and dreary that his long-term relationship with Britten appears puzzling and unsatisfactory. What would Britten's music have been like without Pears? How would Pears's voice have developed without Britten? Did they stifle each other's talents or was this indeed one of the great artistic partnerships of the century? Apart from satisfying our impertinent curiosity, do we need to know more about how their relationship actually worked? It's easy to answer 'no' and slam shut the closet door, but one of the things Britten learnt from Auden in the thirties was the importance of using personal and private subtexts to fuel the engine of public and political artistic creativity. In Britten's case, homosexuality and paedophilia fuel the drama of much of his operatic output and can scarcely be glossed over if his theatrical work is to be understood. Much of what follows is concerned with exploring that private subtext.

What I have not attempted here is any detailed musical analysis. I treat the operas as dramas, taking the libretti seriously as dramatic texts and relating to the music in what it seems to be saying rather than how it says it. In addition to plays for the theatre, I have written two original opera libretti, *Tornrak* for John Metcalf (Welsh National Opera, 1990) and *Cullercoats Tommy* for Eddie McGuire (Northern Sinfonia and Northern Stage, 1993), and worked with Jeremy Sams on a new libretto for Chabrier's *The Reluctant King* for Opera North, (1994). (I've written a full account of my first opera commission in *Outlaw in the Hills*, Methuen, 1991). I came to the conclusion early on that librettists are the true phantoms of the opera, blamed when things go wrong and sidelined at the merest hint of success. The truth is that the librettist has little control over what text the composer finally decides to set or the order in which he, and it generally is still a 'he' (why?), sets it. Composers are at liberty to add in their own lines and change yours at will, occasionally to ridiculous effect, and even write their own, sometimes daft, scenes without consulting the librettist. I am keenly interested in Britten's relationship with his librettists and the manner in which he worked with them. His choice of librettists is odd, with no major dramatist in sight. Poets, a theatre director, a journalist, a novelist and an intelligent friend were his living collaborators. Of course, an opera is the composer's creation, not the librettist's, but any composer, however talented, who fails to use the best resources at his or her disposal is likely to pay the price sooner or later. And a librettist, with years of theatrical experience, an innate understanding of the needs and possibilities of opera and a keen ear for what is singable, is a prime resource.

Finally, my thanks to Peter Burton, a brilliant source of information about gay culture, and for his gift of David Rees's book *Words and Music* (Millivres Books, 1993); to Donald Mitchell for his gift of *Paul Bunyan* (Faber and Faber, 1988); to Peter Stattersfield for access to his formidable library and friendly support; to Duncan Sprott for reading first drafts of my chapters with a sharp eye; and to Nick Drake, the perfect editor.

MICHAEL WILCOX SEPTEMBER 1996

Lumberjacks at no.7

PAUL BUNYAN:
LIBRETTIST W.H. AUDEN, FIRST PERFORMANCE ON 5TH MAY 1941 IN NEW YORK

BENJAMIN BRITTEN
AND W.H. AUDEN
1941

Benjamin Britten and Peter Pears, two criminals under both English and American State law on account of their homosexual relationship, shared a room on the third floor of that adventure playground for artists, presided over by the schoolmasterly W.H. Auden, 7 Middagh Street, Brooklyn, New York. They moved there in November 1941, and Britten celebrated his 27th birthday on the 22nd of that month, St Cecilia's Day. Other tenants of this extraordinary household included Paul Bowles, Louis MacNeice, Carson McCullers, Gypsy Rose Lee and, after Britten's departure, Salvador Dali. Auden himself was living with the young Chester Kallman, who was to celebrate his 20th birthday the following January. During his stay, Pears was so badly bitten by bed bugs that his feet turned septic, necessitating a minor operation. Golo Mann, son of Thomas, joined the Brooklyn household for a while in 1940 and describes life there in his contribution to *W.H. Auden*, a tribute edited by Stephen Spender (Weidenfeld and Nicolson, 1974).

> *'Auden was a stern head of a family. He kept order in the house. there were two coloured servants, who cleaned and cooked the meals – formal, heavy meals which were eaten in a gloomy basement with plush covered furniture. If anyone was late, Auden did not conceal his disapproval. Expenses were covered in accordance with a complicated system thought out by Auden; all subscribed to a general domestic economy, and there were individual prices for each meal. It was a serious question how many meals anyone had missed, after due notification in advance. Once a week there was a 'bill-day', announced with a certain satisfaction by Auden at breakfast time; afterwards he went from room to room collecting payment.'*

Auden sounds more like a tyrannical Brighton landlady than the Lord of Misrule in a bohemian commune, but the fussy order he imposed may have contributed to the artistic productivity of the household. While he and Britten worked on *Paul Bunyan*, Gypsy Rose Lee was taking time off stripping to write her novel, *The G-String Murders,* and, from Paul Bowles's autobiography of 1972, *Without Stopping,* it appears that Carson McCullers was already planning *A Member of the Wedding* which wasn't published until 1946.

By the time of his first meeting with Peter Pears in February 1934 during rehearsals of *A Boy was Born* with the BBC Singers, Britten, then aged twenty-four, was already a busy and recently published composer. But it was not until 1937 that his friendship with the young tenor developed, and in May 1939 they decided to follow Auden and Isherwood across the Atlantic when war with Germany seemed inevitable and imminent. According to Pears, it wasn't until June 1939, when he stayed the night with Britten in a hotel on University Avenue, Toronto, (Pears and Britten landed in Canada) that their relationship achieved a new intensity, culminating four days later, at Grand Rapids, Michigan, in full consummation with Britten the passive partner.

Britten had 'an operetta for children' in mind at least as early as his arrival in North America and it was his natural decision to approach W.H. Auden for a libretto. The composer and Auden, who was already resident in America, had collaborated ever since the GPO Film Unit brought them together in 1935. In addition to the notable documentaries, *Coal Face* and *Night Mail,* Britten had written music for the Auden and Isherwood plays *The Ascent of F6* and *On the Frontier,* and had set Auden's poems to music in *Look, Stranger!* and the amazing *Our Hunting Fathers* in 1936, and in *On this Island* the following year. The result of their latest collaboration was to be 'a new operetta in two acts', premièred at the Brander Mathews Hall, New York in May 1941: *Paul Bunyan* was to be loosely based on exploits of the eponymous American folk hero.

Years later, Auden admitted, 'I knew nothing whatever about opera or what is required of a librettist. In consequence, some very lovely music of Britten's went down the drain . . .' After the dust had settled on the première, with its mixed critical reception, Britten, who must have been aware of the dramatic, if not poetic, shortcomings of Auden's libretto, commented, 'I feel I have learned what not to write for the theatre.' Indeed, the composer was to demonstrate over and over again that his dramatic instincts were infinitely greater than the poet's, although Auden had obviously learnt many lessons from *Paul Bunyan* by the time he and Chester Kallman came to work with Stravinsky on *The Rake's Progress* (1951), with Henze on *The Bassarids* (1966) and Nicolas Nabokov on *Love's Labour's Lost* (1973).

The dismissive comments of *Paul Bunyan*'s creators do scant justice to what is an original and brilliant work. True, it lacks a convincing dramatic and narrative structure, and by standards that Britten was to set in his future operas, the characters are conceived with minimal psychological depth. But that said, Britten's first opera is brim-full with marvellous music and Auden provides crisp and memorable texts for the individual numbers.

The mythic Paul Bunyan is a giant in both stature and personality. So large, in fact, that he is represented by his disembodied speaking voice throughout the opera, giving his interventions a god-like *gravitas*. His exploits are related by a hillbilly narrator, who explains, for example, where Tiny, who is the only member of the Bunyan household to appear in the flesh, has come from. A group of lumberjacks in a virgin land needs to wield the axe to create a new civilization. The basic essentials of adequate food, shelter and order are required to liberate the energies of the new settlers towards more diverse and intellectual pursuits. Seen as a creation myth for the New World, with rational materialism rather than divine inspiration as its original life force, *Paul Bunyan* becomes one of the most ambitious and deadly serious 'operettas' in history.

Intended, curiously, both for high school and Broadway performance, Britten ensured that his music was technically within the reach of amateur music theatre performers rather than opera singers and a professional orchestra. In this, as in many other details of what is a deceptively complex score, he creates what would prove to be a testing ground for many devices that he would develop in future operas. Thus the voice of Paul Bunyan foreshadows the voice of Noye; the function of narrator is developed in the roles of Male and Female Chorus in *The Rape of Lucretia*; a young man on a bicycle rides on stage again in *Albert Herring*; the cats Moppet and Poppet are close cousins of the nieces in *Peter Grimes*; Bunyan's Return finds an answering echo in the liturgical drama of the *War Requiem* ('Bugles sang . . .'); the rhythmic patterns of the Mock Funeral March are mirrored in the closing madrigal of *A Midsummer Night's Dream*; the stammering John Shears, with echoes of Vasek in *The Bartered Bride* and cruel comedy here, becomes a truly tragic device in *Billy Budd*; and the use of chorus as protagonist is developed to supreme dramatic heights in *Peter Grimes* and *Billy Budd*. The seeds of future greatness are present in an advanced state of germination.

If *Paul Bunyan* heralds achievements yet to come, it also demonstrates how the young Britten had absorbed the influences of composers past and present. Generally, this is not as parody or imitation, although the Cooks' Duet is indeed a *bel canto* spoof, but shows how the composer has developed his own individual voice from a host of sources. The Old Trees in the Prologue sing an original hymn like an Anglican congregation (later to be a much-used Britten device); the lumberjacks' entry number is a knees-up in the American post-Gilbert and Sullivan tradition; the bluesy 'Gold in the North . . .' owes much to Gershwin, while Carl Orff struts his stuff in the Food Chorus; the Ravel of *l'Enfant et les Sortilèges* is not far away in Fido's Sympathy, and in Bunyan's Goodnight both Ravel and Bartók are at his elbow. Then there's Stravinsky, Weill, the English Ballad Operas, Purcell, and isn't that Mussorgsky in the Mock Funeral March as well? This capacity to assimilate other composers without merely imitating them was present as long ago as his *Four French Songs,* a superb and mature masterpiece completed by Britten when he was a fourteen-year-old schoolboy.

In addition to the public face of *Paul Bunyan* there is a private subtext.

Auden was a more dominant collaborator than Britten would ever tolerate again. Auden the great poet, the guru, the leader of the pack, the mischievous queen, fiercely jealous of the promiscuous Kallman. Auden, prematurely old, lording it over the Peter Pan composer who would never lose touch with his boyishness. Auden, the schoolmaster, expecting all the boys in his class to pay attention. But during the preparation of the new operetta, Britten's relationship with Peter Pears was increasingly consolidated, laying foundations for what was to be a lifelong partnership. As the singer's influence increased, that of the poet-teacher diminished.

'BUT ONCE IN A WHILE THE ODD THING HAPPENS,
ONCE IN A WHILE THE DREAM COMES TRUE,
AND THE WHOLE PATTERN OF LIFE IS ALTERED
ONCE IN A WHILE THE MOON TURNS BLUE.'

At a public level, this is about Paul Bunyan, but also 'That was Peter . . .', as Britten later acknowledged, remembering that night at Grand Rapids. The personal subtext of this beautifully lyrical outburst, coming as it does in the Prologue of his first stage work, is evidence that a gay ambience is present from the start. Similarly, isn't 'Inkslinger's Regret' (the operetta's numbers have individual titles) also a personal reflection of Auden himself?

'ALL THE LITTLE BROOKS OF LOVE
RUN DOWN TOWARDS EACH OTHER.
SOMEWHERE EVERY VALLEY ENDS,
AND LONELINESS IS OVER.
SOME MEET EARLY, SOME MEET LATE,
SOME, LIKE ME, HAVE LONG TO WAIT.'

Chester Kallman was never, and never would be, for Auden what Pears was for Britten, even though the American boy, with many excursions that wounded the older Englishman, stayed with Auden for life. For Auden, the moon never would turn blue, and he knew it. Earlier, Inkslinger sings:

'I LEARNED A PROSE STYLE FROM THE PREACHER
AND THE FACTS OF LIFE FROM THE HENS,
AND FELL IN LOVE WITH THE TEACHER
WHOSE LOVE FOR JOHN KEATS WAS INTENSE.'

The gender of 'the teacher' as well as the nature of the 'love' is deliberately ambiguous.

'THE COMPANY I HAVE TO SPEAK TO
ARE WONDERFUL MEN IN THEIR WAY,
BUT THE THINGS THAT DELIGHT ME ARE GREEK TO
THE JACKS WHO HAUL LUMBER ALL DAY.'

The gay ambience of 'Inkslinger's Song' is unmistakable from a present-day perspective, as it must have been, at the very least, to Auden's inner circle at the time. Isn't this an example of what Paul Bunyan later describes as the 'Love we are ashamed to feel'?

On a more trivial level, Ben Benny, the cook who produces nothing but beans, sounds like a private joke at Britten's expense from the annals of 7 Middagh Street, as does the tantrum Ben Benny throws when he and Sam are dismissed:

'NOT A WORD OF THANKS . . . TREATING US LIKE DOGS . . . YOU DON'T KNOW HOW MUCH YOU'VE HURT US. ONE DAY PERHAPS YOU'LL REALIZE WHAT YOU'VE DONE!'

Exit one young composer and his bruised ego.

Never again would Britten set a libretto with such a weak narrative, or one so structurally flawed. Not the least of the problems was expecting singers to act their spoken lines convincingly. All opera-goers will know what to expect, a post-Gilbertian, all-purpose delivery of speech, that on a good day might win a prize in an elocution class for clarity of diction, but which, from an acting point of view, is hopelessly compromised. The dilemma of choosing between singers who can't act and actors who can't sing bedevils music theatre to this day. In Auden's case, matters were further confounded by the great poet's apparent lack of ear for dialogue. Thus, on the arrival of Tiny, he resorts to a cloying parody of the Seven Dwarfs meeting Snow White, from Walt Disney's classic of 1938:

PETE	I NEVER KNEW HE HAD A DAUGHTER.
ANDY	SHE'S MUCH LOVELIER THAN I THOUGHT HER.
JEN	TINY, WHAT A PRETTY NAME.
CROSS	I AM DELIGHTED THAT SHE CAME.
PETE	HER EYES,
JEN	HER CHEEKS,
CROSS	HER LIPS,
ANDY	HER NOSE.
JEN	SHE'S A PEACH,
JOHN	A DOVE,
PETE	A ROSE.

Sometimes Britten tries to help matters along by using melodrama, underpinning dialogue with music. Indeed, his ability to turn on a sixpence with unflagging musical imagination, even when Auden is at his most puerile, is one of the marvels of the piece.

Its dramatic deficiencies are emphatically not a good reason for consigning *Paul Bunyan* to the history books. If there is one Britten opera that can benefit from an interventionist stage production, this is it. Britten purists turn away while the rest of us imagine a production set in 7 Middagh Street in 1941 and performed by its tenants and visitors. MacNeice is Inkslinger, Pears is Slim and, in this fanciful production, Paul Bowles is Helson. It's tempting to exploit Gypsy Rose Lee as Tiny, but Carson McCullers, whose first novel, *The Heart is a Lonely Hunter,* was to be published in 1940, was little older than the young Chester Kallman and would be a more appropriate casting. Britten and Kallman, the two toy boys of the household, are the 'two bad cooks', Ben Benny and Sam Sharkey. Instead of (to these ears) the tedious hillbilly, the production uses settings that Britten made in 1974 for the boys' choir of the Narrator's songs. These are sung by the half-starved chorus and rent boys who surely partied at No.7. And Auden (who else?) plays Paul Bunyan. The creation myth is played out as spontaneous socially conscious music theatre against a background of Roosevelt's New Deal. Its dramatic possibilities are greatly enhanced by combining the public, private and historic contexts of this hybrid work.

In his detailed programme notes to the only available recording (Virgin Classic's VCD 7 90710-2), Donald Mitchell describes how Britten was persuaded to return his attention to *Paul Bunyan* after his disastrous heart operation. Amongst the revisions that the composer made in 1974, all of which are listed by Mitchell, was the soprano Tiny's coda to her song 'Whether the sun shines upon children playing . . .' The effect is to render these memorable lines sung by the chorus inaudible:

'THE WHITE BONE

LIES ALONE

LIKE THE LIMESTONE

UNDER THE GREEN GRASS.

AS TIME GOES BY

WE TOO SHALL LIE

UNDER DEATH'S EYE.

ALAS, ALAS.'

Britten, of all composers, was acutely sensitive to words, their colours, shades of meaning, complexities of rhythms. By adding Tiny's coda and rendering Auden's bleak lines unintelligible, was the dying man trying to outstare 'death's eye'?

Queer fish

PETER GRIMES:
LIBRETTIST MONTAGU SLATER, FIRST PERFORMANCE ON 7TH JUNE 1945 AT
SADLER'S WELLS, LONDON

MONTAGU SLATER

'This way for Peter Grimes, the sadistic fisherman!' as the north London bus conductor famously instructed his passengers. 'If you want a noise, Britten can make it,' was also a cheap catch phrase of the time. A degree of personal antagonism towards the young composer and his partner on their return to wartime England was not altogether surprising. They were both 'conchies' (conscientious objectors) at a time of total war. If public perception of them had included their 'queerness', then arrest, imprisonment and humiliation as criminals, or even as 'moral imbeciles' under the iniquitous and much abused Mental Deficiency Act of 1913, could have been their fate, as it already had been for countless anonymous homosexuals, in addition to an even greater number of unmarried mothers. Nor had their departure for America in 1939 occasioned much sympathy, and anyway, by the time the *Axel Johnson* docked at Liverpool on 17th April 1942, cynics might have wrongly observed that the most dangerous period of the war was over.

There were at least three reasons why they returned when they did. Britten was homesick for Suffolk, he had an urgent and exciting project in the new opera to complete, and, importantly, America had afforded him the time and space to define the relationship that would provide him with some personal stability, as well as professional inspiration, for the rest of his life. After setting up homes for himself and Pears in Suffolk and London, Britten got to work on numerous projects, including incidental music, premièred in 1943, for radio drama, in addition to *Rejoice in the Lamb* Op. 30, and *Serenade* Op. 31 for tenor, horn and strings.

An unusual glimpse of Britten in wartime England is offered by June Mahon, then a teenager living in the ground floor flat of Spanish Place Mansions in Manchester Square, not far from the Wigmore Hall, with her doctor father and mother. The basement apartment was occupied by actor Elwyn Brook-Jones and his wife. Elwyn had trained as a concert pianist in his youth and possessed an excellent piano. Britten was a frequent visitor and young June Mahon spent hours listening to him while he played.

'You know, what people don't realize is that Ben, when he wanted to be, was a wonderful swing pianist. A great favourite was 'Don't Fence Me In!' . . . you know . . . Cole Porter . . . He must have learnt it in America. He could really let his hair down! Our first real meeting with Ben was hilarious! On the top floor lived a reclusive Scot called Howgrave-Graham . . . he was the private secretary to the head of the Metropolitan Police. Anyway, about 9 a.m. on a Sunday morning, daddy, who was taking in our milk, heard a stricken voice down the lift shaft. "Dr Mahon . . . help . . . help me!" Up we all rushed to find that Mr Graham had been shut out of his flat on the way to the bathroom. The door had slammed and there he was, poor man, in his birthday suit with nothing but a rusty fire hydrant to cover his modesty. Ben rushed up from the basement . . . he often stayed for nights on end . . . and joined in the hilarity. Daddy fetched an enormous dressing-gown and Ben eventually took the poor man down to the basement to await the locksmith. I believe they became friends but one never knew with Howgrave-Graham . . . he was so secretive. Next day, Leslie Boosey . . . you know . . . of Boosey and Hawkes, the music publishers . . . came to lunch. We asked what he thought of Ben's music. "Very odd, but it will catch on eventually."

'I had dreadful measles . . . when was it? . . . in May, I think . . . that's 1943 . . . anyway, Ben used to bring me food sent from America. He really looked after me. We used to go shopping at the British produce store in Wigmore Street . . . the woman on the payout whispered to me; "What's the matter with that man? he keeps telling me to go to the opera!" Ben always insisted on carrying everything. He was so kind and generous. We couldn't really understand his music, but when he played we were mesmerized. We hardly ever saw Peter Pears . . . he was always away, singing somewhere. I think that's why Ben was round so often. He liked to be fed and made a fuss of.

At the end of the war, we all went to the première of Peter Grimes. *We found Ben wandering the street outside Sadler's Wells, looking green and terrified. We tried to cheer him up, but he was inconsolable and refused to enter the theatre. The atmosphere inside was tense and thrilling, but we didn't much like the new opera. We all clapped like mad, anyway!'*

Returning to 1942 and the homecoming of the prodigals, the scenario for what was to prove one of the great operas of the twentieth century was already sketched out amongst their luggage, along with the exquisite 'A Ceremony of Carols', composed, amazingly, during the hazardous journey across the Atlantic. The idea for the new opera had been triggered by E.M. Forster's radio broadcast, printed in *The Listener*, 'George Crabbe: the Poet and the Man', with its graphic descriptions of the sights and sounds of the Suffolk coastline where Britten had spent his childhood. The poems were sought out and devoured, and Crabbe's cruel fisherman, haunted by the ghosts of his dead apprentices and their vengeful father, was irresistible operatic material. Christopher Isherwood turned down the job of librettist, Peter Pears was considered, but eventually Britten decided on Montagu Slater, a journalist for whose Left Theatre plays Britten had written incidental music in the thirties. Koussevitzky generously commissioned the piece and it was scheduled provisionally for production at the 1944 Berkshire Music Festival in Massachusetts.

Britten had learnt some of the basic rules of any successful new opera from the bitter experience of working with Auden on *Paul Bunyan*. It's the composer's opera, not the librettist's. Get the libretto right before starting to compose the music. Britten's brilliant contemporary, Michael Tippett, might learn to prefer to write his own words and music together, but that would be his own idiosyncratic method. Montagu Slater, working from the ideas and sketches that Britten gave him, as well as from Crabbe's poems, produced a highly theatrical draft. If this differed from the libretto that Britten finally set – without, for example, the ghosts of the dead boys – Slater offered his composer a most colourful and dramatically aware starting point. He displayed that essential librettist's talent of hearing the musical possibilities of what he was writing before a note had actually been composed. His libretto possessed a strong storyline, vivid characters and sufficient dramatic energy to ensure that the piece would be effective even with a composer less talented than Britten. In this respect, Slater demonstrated all the librettist's skills that Auden had lacked.

But others were at hand to influence the way the libretto developed. Peter Pears had become an important operatic tenor with Sadler's Wells Opera Company, singing Tamino, Alfredo, the Duke in *Rigoletto* and the stammering Vasek in *The Bartered Bride*. The way his distinctive voice had developed, to say nothing of his inspirational acting ability, surprised and delighted everyone. Grimes was to have been a baritone, but Britten soon saw, quite correctly, what an ideal part it would be for his partner.

Crucial decisions had to be made about what sort of man Grimes really was, especially if Pears was to play him. Sadist? Pederast? Psychopath? Serial killer? Gradually, a new focus was pulled on what was now the tenor lead. Grimes would be an outsider, a visionary, an idealist driven to madness and suicide by an uncaring, uncomprehending society. This chimed in well with the personal situations of composer and singer, alienated on account of their pacifism and homosexuality. But it was no longer Montagu Slater's Peter Grimes, let alone Crabbe's. After the première, Slater published his version of the libretto as a dramatic poem in its own right. Britten's final libretto was tweaked and further adapted by himself, Pears and, importantly, the opera's first director, and one of the composer's future librettists, Eric Crozier.

But does the transformation of Grimes into the misunderstood victim of an uncomprehending and vicious society work? Let's set aside Slater and Crabbe and the much written about genesis of the work and examine the evidence of what is actually there in *Peter Grimes,* the opera. The crucial event is what has happened before the action starts in the prologue's courtroom. A boy has died in circumstances that demand a coroner's inquest. Grimes claims that, when he and his young apprentice, William Spode, netted a huge catch of fish, he decided to sail round the coast to London to sell it. The wind blew the boat off course, they ran out of drinking water and the boy died. This explanation begs too many questions to be believed. It takes many days, if not weeks, to die from lack of water. Time enough to find harbour somewhere along the coast, even in bad weather. Time to make contact with other boats, or, for heaven's sake, live off the fish.

A stage direction tells us that Justice Swallow, the coroner, is 'a man of unexceptional career and talents', and one can see why. Grimes admits that he and the boy were at sea for only three days, hardly time in which to die of thirst with a loaded boat. Grimes then testifies that on the boy's death, he threw the catch overboard. He might have argued, had Swallow the sense to question him further, that by so doing the boat would sail faster back to port. But equally, it makes it impossible to verify whether there was ever a huge catch in the first place.

Grimes admits that the first person he contacted on returning to the Borough with the body was Ned Keene, described in the cast list as 'apothecary and quack'. In addition to supplying drugs to the community in the form of laudanum (liquid opium), we learn in the next scene that Keene supplies boys from the workhouse to Grimes. Why does he do this? It is clear that there has been overwhelming hostility towards Grimes long before William Spode met his highly suspicious end. The inference behind this hostility is that Grimes abuses the boys in his care. At the inquest, Grimes wants to 'stop people's mouths . . . The charges that no court has made will be shouted at my head.' Spode may be the first boy to die in his charge, but unspecified events, described euphemistically as Grimes's 'exercise' are common gossip in the neighbourhood. The implication is that the community believes that Grimes has abused other boys before his contact with the unfortunate William Spode. We are not told why the other apprentices left Grimes's service or what has become of them.

The precise nature of what happens when 'Grimes is at his exercise' affects our attitude towards him. Grimes himself would have us believe that nothing happens, that all is merely malicious rumour. Then there is the suspicion, never fully substantiated by anything in the final text of the libretto, that Grimes either sexually abuses his boys, or that he suppresses his guilty sexual fantasies and resorts to verbal and physical violence towards his young apprentices.

Does the music tell us anything that the text does not? When Ellen Orford, the widow who offers Grimes the possibility of emotional support, finds a bruise on the new boy's neck and rows with Grimes, he strikes her (more evidence of violence) and sings 'And God have mercy upon me!' to the same theme that the chorus used for 'Grimes is at his exercise'. By linking Grimes's 'exercise' music with his plea for divine forgiveness, the music appears to tell us that Grimes acknowledges his guilt, that the rumours have substance, that Grimes does abuse his apprentices.

To underline this revelation, the 'God have mercy' theme then becomes the basis for the orchestral Interlude IV (Passacaglia). In the story, Grimes is driving the poor boy back to his hut so they can fish for a huge shoal that Grimes imagines he sees that Sunday morning. The Passacaglia becomes a vivid account of Grimes's violent and abusive nature. The stage direction at the top of the scene that follows is detailed and specific. Grimes's hut is an upturned boat, bare and forbidding. 'The boy staggers into the room as if thrust from behind.' The blatant sexual image here cannot be brushed aside as accidental. The libretto was years in the making and every detail carefully challenged and scrutinized. It is typical of Britten, as will be seen in subsequent operas, to distance himself from crucial moments that are too explicit, too painful, too precise, too private and personal. In this instance, he distances himself by depicting in music alone what might have been more explicitly dramatized.

Grimes then treats the terrified boy to humiliating threats and abuse. 'Go there! . . . Take those bright and fancy buckles off your feet . . . I'll tear the collar off your neck.' (Jon Vickers, in the Colin Davis recording, changes these lines to: 'That's no way to make things better than they were . . . I'll teach you not to lie to her.' Presumably, Vickers found the original text so incriminating that he felt the characterization of Grimes as misunderstood outsider fell apart at this point.) With the lynch party banging at the door, the terrified boy is bundled out of the back of the hut and falls to his death down the cliff that leads to the sea. Grimes escapes, and when we next encounter him, he appears quite mad with fear, guilt and despair. He needs little persuading to sail his boat out to sea, sink her and drown himself.

Slater's original version of the hut scene is more explicitly brutal, and shows how much Britten eventually toned down the violence:

'BY GOD I'LL BEAT IT OUT OF YOU. STAND UP (LASH) STRAIGHTEN (LASH). I'LL COUNT TWO. AND THEN YOU'LL JUMP TO IT. ONE – WELL? TWO.' (THE BOY DOESN'T MOVE. THEN PETER LASHES HARD, TWICE. HE RUNS. PETER FOLLOWS.)

'YOUR SOUL IS MINE
YOUR BODY IS THE CAT O' NINE
TAILS' MINCEMEAT, O! A PRETTY DISH
SMOOTH-SKINNED & YOUNG AS SHE COULD WISH.
COME CAT! UP WHIPLASH! JUMP MY SON
JUMP (LASH) JUMP (LASH) JUMP, THE DANCE IS ON.'

The precise stage directions, with even the number and timing of lashes the boy receives from Grimes in place, which would generally be added to the libretto either during rehearsal or after the first production, are an additional curiosity, suggesting theatrical inexperience on Slater's part.

In his radio broadcast of 1974, Peter Pears tried hard to justify his perception that Grimes was not a sadist or an abuser; 'I don't think he's a sadist at all . . . the helpless and incompetent can very easily arouse irritation . . . men are frequently brutal when infuriated . . . Grimes . . . is madly irritated by the child's weakness and slowness . . .' Oddly, Pears seems to think William Spode 'drowned in a rough sea', while, in fact, he died of thirst, ' . . . lying there among the fish . . .' while Grimes looked on, as Grimes himself testifies to the coroner's court. Pears's attempt to explain away Grimes's heartless conduct as comprehensible male behaviour, to say nothing of bending the facts to suit his case, makes one gasp with disbelief. Listening to Britten's own recording for Decca, the viciousness of Pears's portrayal of Grimes as abuser in the hut scene is truly harrowing. We hear the boy whimpering with terror, the boots and oilskins flung at him and his terrible scream as he falls to his death. The stage directions are also explicit: 'He throws the clothes at the boy . . . the boy is crying silently. Peter shakes his shoulder . . . he tears off the boy's coat and throws the jersey at him . . . he gives the boy a shove which knocks him over. He [the boy] lies sobbing miserably . . .' Britten, the conductor, endorses these graphic stage directions in his recording. Grimes ignores the boy's misery and bullies him in a sustained and merciless fashion, breaking off only to muse on how better things might be if Ellen was part of the household. If this isn't sadistic, what is?

Is there any sense in which the argument for Grimes as visionary, idealist or victim can be sustained? His entry into 'The Boar' at the height of the storm and his extraordinary solo 'Now the Great Bear and Pleiades . . .' is indeed a vision beyond time and space, posing insoluble questions:

'WHO CAN DECIPHER

IN STORM OR STARLIGHT

THE WRITTEN CHARACTER

OF A FRIENDLY FATE —

AS THE SKY TURNS THE WORLD FOR US TO CHANGE?

...WHO CAN TURN SKIES BACK AND BEGIN AGAIN?'

Britten sets up this moment with superb dramatic skill. Surely it is one of the greatest theatrical entries in all opera? Elemental power is unleashed outside in the storm and from within the psyche of a deranged man. This is the outpouring of someone with quite different perceptions of the universe from those around him. Grimes certainly has his visionary moments, but Grimes the idealist is more difficult to pin down. Yes, he sees through the hypocrisy of his isolated community, who pretend to be so godly while doping on opium and whoring with Auntie and her nieces, but that doesn't add up to idealism, and he is at least as dysfunctional as the rest of them, and more dangerously so.

Grimes as victim? Viewed from our perspective, he's a sick man. He needs psychiatric care not available in nineteenth-century Suffolk. The reason most of the Borough rejects him is that he's a danger to boys, not because he sees visions in the pub or fishes on a Sunday. If Justice Swallow hadn't been such a dimwit at the inquest, and insisted that Grimes should use a much older lad in future (one is tempted to say a lad beyond the age of consent), the tragic outcome might have been prevented. In the event, the true victim of society in the opera is not Grimes but the boy, 'a workhouse brat' to Captain Balstrode, or, more sinisterly, to the procurer Keene 'your bargain' and 'his purchase'. While the Borough sings its pious psalms and offers up its hollow prayers, it condones apprenticeship bordering on child slavery. The workhouse boy has no rights and is supposed to be grateful for the upturned boat over his head, a world upside down.

And what an odd bunch the other characters are. Ellen Orford and Mrs Sedley are widows, the latter being 'a rentier widow of an East India Company factor', and all the men appear to be unmarried. Captain Balstrode, a retired merchant skipper, has seen a thing or two of the world, yet it is he who tells Grimes to go and drown himself 'out of sight of the Moot Hall'. Auntie at 'The Boar' is a madam and her two nieces whores. Bob Boles, both fisherman and Methodist minister, can't control his sexual urges after a couple of drinks. Rev. Horace Adams, Church of England rector, leads the mob to Grimes's hut. It is his resounding knock that finally causes the boy to flee through the cliff door to his death. And, as we have seen, Justice Swallow is dull and pompous, while Ned Keene supplies the Borough with boys and drugs. In addition to being single, all are at least middle-aged. The Borough seems bereft of young people apart from those procured from the workhouse or working as 'nieces'. It is a society heading for extinction, like an unstable cliff being undermined by the pounding of the ocean. And how extraordinary that such a work should triumph with audiences in a starving, blitzed and bankrupt country at the end of five years of total war.

'The more vicious the society, the more vicious the individual,' commented Britten before the first New York Metropolitan Opera production. Not necessarily, one is tempted to counter-challenge, risking another tantrum from 'Ben Benny', the Britten parody in *Paul Bunyan*. Vicious societies have produced more saints than benign ones. What Britten and Pears were doing, by creating this image of Grimes as an outsider destroyed by an unsympathetic and sick society, was deflecting attention from the true storm at the centre of Britten's life, which finds surrogate expression in this opera and elsewhere, namely his own passion for boys.

In researching his biography of the composer, Humphrey Carpenter interviewed a number of men who knew and worked with Britten as boys. The composite image that their remarkably frank accounts create is of a man trapped somewhere between desire and fulfilment, longing to taste what he dare not touch. A doting generosity and kindliness substitutes for sensual gratification. The fate of the apprentices in *Peter Grimes* must have affected him deeply. Where he, as one outsider, would shower attention and concern, fussing over his boys at bedtime like a mischievous granny, the outsider in the opera was the complete opposite, directing with careless violence all his anger and frustration at his small and defenceless apprentices. The ambiguities in the title role – social, political and sexual – present a supreme challenge to all its interpreters. But any artist who assumes the sanitized characterization described in that confused radio interview by Peter Pears will only tell half the story. A better starting point might be to heed the judgement of the conductor of the No. 19 bus.

Rape in the night

THE RAPE OF LUCRETIA:

LIBRETTIST RONALD DUNCAN, FIRST PERFORMANCE ON 7TH JUNE 1946

AT GLYNDEBOURNE OPERA HOUSE

'He told me he had been raped by a master at his school, as if his sexual deviation had stemmed from that one incident . . .' Eric Crozier was putting the record straight about aspects of his working relationship with Britten in 1966 in irritation at his exclusion from Imogen Holst's recent biography of the composer. Humphrey Carpenter investigates this claim thoroughly in his biography with inconclusive results. What the composer was possibly trying to tell Crozier was not that this experience had turned a heterosexual into a homosexual, but that this childhood violation, whatever 'rape' actually meant, had stunted his natural homosexual development and made him a paedophile, forever seeking ways to love boys of the age at which he was 'raped' without, in turn, abusing them.

The delicacy of Britten's personal experience may account both for his attraction to a famous historical rape for his next opera, as well as, paradoxically, the various devices that he and his new librettist, the playwright and poet Ronald Duncan, used to distance themselves from their subject. After the psychological complexities and tantalizing ambiguities of *Peter Grimes,* with its hot-blooded theatricality, *The Rape of Lucretia,* for all the brilliance and beauty of its score, seems dramatically desiccated. The story of the young Prince Tarquinius's nocturnal ride from his army barracks to the house of Lucretia to seduce, or if needs be, rape her, has great dramatic potential. Lucretia, famed and mocked for her virtue, is sexually humiliated and driven to suicide in spite of her husband, Collotinus, in no way holding her to blame for what happened. 'Spirit (Lucretia) defiled by fate' (Tarquinius) is Duncan's summation of the opera. Admirable artistic ambition is sadly compromised in its realization, however.

BENJAMIN BRITTEN AND RONALD DUNCAN AT GLYNDEBOURNE, 1946

What went wrong? Certainly not the bold idea to establish 'a living school of British opera'. By abandoning the massive resources needed for traditional operatic productions, Britten resolved to use just eight singers and a chamber orchestra of twelve. The clarity of texture would allow every word of the libretto to be heard, even, so it would prove on tour after the initial fourteen performances at Glyndebourne, in the largest venues. The new opera received no less than eighty-three consecutive performances, using two complete casts. And fortunate were those who saw the 'B team' in action, with the great Aksel Schiotz in the Pears' role of Male Chorus and Nancy Evans as Lucretia. The young, and, at the time, relatively unknown Kathleen Ferrier sang the title role with Pears and Joan Cross in the 'A team'. Coupled with John Piper sets and Eric Crozier directing, fresh from the triumph of his *Peter Grimes* production, there was no shortage of talent in depth. And out of this enlightened, if finally compromised, production would grow the English Opera Group which would, in turn, give birth to some of this century's most inspired and durable operatic projects.

In its review of extracts recorded by members of these original casts shortly after the première, *The Record Guide* (Collins, 1951) lists features of the opera that 'have militated against the success of the work'. These include 'an overtly Christian commentary on the action . . . wilful misaccenting of the name Collatinus, inappropriate jokes' and 'absurd anachronisms'. Listening to Decca's 1970 complete recording, conducted by the composer (LONDON 425 666–2), one wonders what on earth the 'inappropriate jokes' were that antagonized those first audiences. Could it be that parts of Duncan's libretto were so laughable that audiences supposed these 'jokes' to be deliberate?

There are reviews in the *Penguin Music Magazine* of 1947 of both the Glyndebourne première and the same production on tour in Manchester. Of the première, Stephen Williams writes that 'the highly expressive singing of Peter Pears and Joan Cross saved the Male and Female Chorus from becoming a couple of sententious bores'. He praises 'the brilliant musicianship and rather austere beauty' of the opera. J.H. Elliot in Manchester, however, has a different story to tell:

> *'The general impression was that Britten had strayed, or allowed himself to be led, into an operatic blind alley . . . while the music of Lucretia has all the originality and expertness . . . that we expect from its brilliant young composer, it somehow misses the uncanny truth and spiritual integration of the Peter Grimes score. The difficulty, it seemed, lay primarily in the experimental dramatic form with its quasi-Greek choruses and super-abundance of bald narrative and commentary.'*

The libretto was therefore seen as being the opera's weakest component from the outset, but it is unreasonable to apportion the entire blame for this to Ronald Duncan. 'The composer and poet should at all stages be working in close contact, from preliminary stages right up to the first night,' wrote Britten in *The Rape of Lucretia: A Symposium* (Bodley Head, 1948). And, on this occasion, that's exactly what happened. In the same book, Duncan describes how he and the composer worked at the same desk, planning out the dramatic and musical structure of each scene and drafting and redrafting the libretto together. They used André Obey's play of 1931, *Le Viol de Lucrece,* as their prime source (a source insufficiently acknowledged in the Bodley Head *Symposium*), condensing its four acts into two. If Auden had played the dominant role in *Paul Bunyan* and many hands had been employed in fashioning the final libretto of *Peter Grimes*, this time the composer was working as one with a collaborator who would, in the last resort, do what he was told.

It was Britten, for example, who wanted and got the much-criticized Christian perspective on this pre-Christian story. Why? There is a long English tradition, stretching back to the Anglo-Saxon poems 'The Wanderer' and 'The Seafarer', in which pagan art is first adopted and then redefined in a Christian context, providing an established precedent for Britten's decision. Without the Christian moral, the opera would have ended on a note of utter nihilism, with all the soloists singing:

'HOW IS IT POSSIBLE THAT SHE
BEING SO PURE SHOULD DIE?
HOW IS IT POSSIBLE THAT WE
GRIEVING FOR HER SHOULD LIVE?
SO BRIEF IS BEAUTY
IS THIS IT ALL? IT IS ALL! IT IS ALL!'

Having taken us to the brink of the abyss, Britten either lacked the guts or the commitment to leave us there. Was he worried by the possible reaction of his orthodox, middle-class opera audience and feared their rejection? Or was he, as an artist, expressing his profoundly felt Christian optimism? Sadly, one suspects that Britten sugared the pill to appease his audience.

The busy roles of Male and Female Chorus, who set the scenes, link the narrative, provide historical background, externalize the inner motivation of some of the characters and provide the Christian wrapping, are borrowed and developed from Obey's play. They are required by the libretto to read from books like crusty old pedants, and we can see them doing just that in the original production photographs. These pivotal roles are so substantial, while not being characters directly involved in the drama of the narrative, that they are constantly intervening between the audience and the true focus of the drama. Describing something at second hand, even as vividly as the justly famous sequence of Tarquinius's ride through the night, is not the same thing as providing the audience with the direct experience of the ride itself. Britten and Duncan were confusing the concert hall oratorio tradition, dramatic enough in its way, for theatrical drama. Even though there is a tradition of messengers and choruses describing crucial off-stage action in Greek and Roman plays, so what? This is an opera written during eight months of 1946 in a half-starved country, shattered by war and now experiencing bread rationing for the first time, and not some disinterred theatrical monster from the past.

Ronald Duncan had helped Britten with the text of the final scene of *Peter Grimes*. In 1945 he had achieved publicity and some acclaim for his turgid verse play *This Way to the Tomb* for which Britten wrote the incidental music. With Christopher Fry and others, he was part of a movement to reintroduce verse drama to the British stage. In the same year that he was working with Britten on *The Rape of Lucretia,* Duncan premièred his new stage play *The Eagle has Two Heads*. In British theatre of the day, Duncan, an almost forgotten figure now, was at the centre of attention. A few examples of his versifying in the libretto demonstrate, sadly, that this emperor had no clothes.

'SATED, THE SUN FALLS THROUGH THE HORIZON, THE AIR
SITS ON THEIR BACKS LIKE A HEAVY BEAR.'

Like 'a heavy bear'? Why, even, 'a bear'? A bear of modest size would quite easily squash someone flat if it sat on his or her back. It's a preposterous image. The only reason for introducing the 'bear' seems to be that it rhymes with 'air'.

'THE OATMEAL SLIPPERS OF SLEEP
CREEP THROUGH THE CITY . . .'

'Oatmeal slippers of sleep'? What on earth is an 'oatmeal slipper'? No doubt, there is probably an obscure answer, but there isn't time in an opera to puzzle it out.

When the rampant Tarquinius has entered the sleeping Lucretia's bedroom (always a tricky moment with singers cast for their voices, not their physical aptitude or acting ability) and kissed her awake, what is the first line that Duncan gives her?

'WHAT DO YOU WANT FROM ME?'

Pity the poor artist having to deliver such an obvious question under the circumstances. (Is this one of *The Record Guide*'s 'inappropriate jokes'?) Did no one in rehearsal challenge such banalities, which are present on every page? Not even Eric Crozier, who must have had the gravest misgivings over the text?

Then, at one of the opera's most moving moments, Lucretia 'is seen walking slowly towards (her husband) Collatinus. She is dressed in purple mourning.' Britten illustrates this with music of tragic beauty, echoing the widowed Andromache's entry with her son Astyanax in Berlioz's *Les Troyens*. Lucretia's first lines to her husband are:

'TO LOVE AS WE LOVED
WAS TO BE NEVER BUT AS MOIETY . . .'

To introduce the word 'moiety', a legal term meaning 'half', in such a context is bound to puzzle those members of the audience who are neither solicitors nor Shakespearean scholars. The music moves on. Most of the audience hasn't got time to figure out what Lucretia actually means, and the virtue of Britten's chamber orchestra and his economic scoring is to render every word audible. Duncan tells us in the Bodley Head *Symposium* that 'it is useless to write a complicated sentence' when writing opera libretti. Sadly, he fails to follow his own advice, confusing, at this key moment, verbal obscurantism for poetic insight.

Britten seems to have been deluded into believing that he was setting dramatic poetry of quality. This is all the more surprising when one remembers the brilliant choice of Christopher Smart's strange poems in *Rejoice in the Lamb,* of Rimbaud in *Les Illuminations,* of Wilfred Owen in the *War Requiem* and the wonderfully eclectic anthologies employed in the *Spring Symphony,* the *Nocturne* for tenor, seven obligato instruments and string orchestra, and in the *Serenade* for tenor, horn and strings. The aptness of the poetry in these marvellous works is perhaps a tribute to the influence of Peter Pears. But in the present opera, one wonders, with composer and poet working so closely together, how many of the libretto's solecisms were inspired by Britten, with Duncan simply writing under instruction.

Is there anything in the music that sheds light on the story of Britten's own experience of rape as a boy? One thing lacking in the music from the moment of Tarquinius's entrance into Lucretia's bedroom until the rape itself is even the remotest hint of eroticism. Observing the sleeping Lucretia by candlelight, Tarquinius sings with all the tenderness of a father watching over a sleeping child. Lucretia is kissed and the spell of magical night music is broken by the crack of a whip. There is an angry exchange, with much demanding and much protesting (excruciating contributions from Duncan), and with the Male and Female Choruses having their say in the proceedings. Finally, at the moment of the rape, the 'front cloth falls quickly', leaving the Male and Female Chorus to chant verses about 'virtue assailed by sin' and to make the parallel between Christ's crucifixion and Lucretia's fate. The music accompanying this is intensely violent rather than explicitly sexual. Curiously, it doesn't reach an orgasmic climax but sinks into exhaustion instead, as though Tarquinius has managed to penetrate Lucretia, who has put up a hell of a fight, but has found himself to be impotent at the point of orgasm. At no point is Britten's music sexually graphic or titillating. Anger and violence are there in plenty, but eroticism not at all. Is this deliberate? Or was Britten, with his own sexual nature focused so sharply on nurturing the affections of pre-pubescent boys, simply out of his depth when trying to depict physical adult heterosexuality?

Or is there another explanation? Is the composer remembering his own trauma and putting that experience at the service of the music? Does that explain the paternal tenderness of Tarquinius's initial response to seeing his sleeping victim? Lucretia's 'What do you want? . . . What do you want from me?' is quite absurd coming from an adult under the circumstances, the answer being so obvious, but not from an innocent child. These are unusually direct and simply worded questions by Duncan's convoluted and image-laden standards. Are these in fact Britten's lines, not the librettist's, and a memory of his own abuse? Is there, lurking in the darkness of Lucretia's bedroom, the shadow of Britten's own father? In an article in the *Guardian* newspaper in February 1991, Tom Sutcliffe suggests that Britten's father was himself a paedophile and the boys that his son brought home were the objects of his sexual interest, making the young Britten 'an implicit procurer'. If this is true, one must surely ask whether his father ever sexually abused young Ben. Are the Christian verses, chanted over the violence and furious bewilderment of the rape, a comprehensible and pitiable response from a child seeking help from 'Our Father which art in Heaven . . .' when his earthly father is raping him?

The most affecting music in the opera comes in its final scene, with Lucretia achieving truly tragic status, and, with echoes of Purcell's Dido, accepting her fate with quiet nobility. For almost the first time, the audience is able to empathize directly with the human emotions of one of the characters in the drama. For all the cleverness and beauties of Britten's score, for too long we have been passive observers, held at arms' length by the persistent interventions of the Male and Female Choruses and the one-dimensional characters. As well as keeping us at arms' length from the action of the drama, is this evidence that Britten was also protecting himself from the bitter memory and destructive legacy of his own rape and abuse, whether at school or at home?

After a performance in 1947, Michael Tippett went backstage to see the composer. Knowing something about Britten's next operatic project, he said, 'If you're now going to write a comic opera, for Christ's sake don't use this librettist.' Mercifully, Britten took Tippett's advice.

Albert comes out

ALBERT HERRING:

LIBRETTIST ERIC CROZIER, FIRST PERFORMANCE 20TH JUNE 1947
BY THE ENGLISH OPERA GROUP AT GLYNDEBOURNE OPERA HOUSE

Albert, the village grocer lad who lives with his mother as the only child in a single-parent family, stands out from the community of Loxford, like a rural, provincial Lucretia, on account of his virtue. Nobody doubts that he's sober and a virgin, which in Loxford is a rare state of grace. It's 1900, the start of a new century, and distant Rome, thank heavens, has given way to homely Suffolk. The establishment, led by the fierce, opinionated and, above all, rich Lady Billows fails to find a suitably chaste village girl to be crowned Queen of the May, and, creating a new precedent, chooses a boy instead. What they have all failed to realize is that young Albert is a time bomb. Albert is homosexual.

Britten's choice of Eric Crozier to adapt Maupassant's short story, 'Le Rosier de Madame Husson' proved a happy one. Crozier had been one of the first television producers at the BBC before joining the Sadler's Wells company as Tyrone Guthrie's assistant. He had directed Pears in *The Bartered Bride* and was delegated to direct *Peter Grimes* by the unwilling Guthrie. Like Britten, he was also a conscientious objector. Crozier's libretto for *Albert Herring* is almost entirely excellent, presenting the composer with a lean and effective comedy, which never quite sinks to farce and in which the serious core of the drama, Albert's sexual liberation, is kept in sharp focus. Crozier manages to characterize his cast of thirteen with swift precision, creating a credible world for the action. No narrators or choruses come between the plot and the audience. There are no tiresome dramatic devices and Crozier demonstrates with ease that often undervalued dramatist's skill of getting his characters on and off stage without obvious contrivance. With today's new theatre writing generally confined to cut-price studio productions, our contemporary playwrights handle casts of three or four with great resourcefulness, while

L–R : FREDERICK ASHTON, ERIC CROZIER, BENJAMIN BRITTEN
AND PETER PEARS, GLYNDEBOURNE, 1947

John Christie, Glyndebourne's inspirational, eccentric owner, was snooty about the brilliant new opera, advising old friends in the audience that this really wasn't their sort of thing.

the skills involved in writing for casts in double figures are in danger of being lost. In 1947, English repertory theatres staged large cast plays on a regular basis, with the same company of actors performing one play in the evenings and rehearsing next week's production during the day. The practical skills learnt by such discipline shine through in Crozier's work.

As with *The Rape of Lucretia,* the new opera was composed in a remarkably short time, with Britten writing some of the music even before the libretto was completed. *Albert Herring,* although scheduled for production at Glyndebourne, was to be the first project of The English Opera Group, and in addition to the writing of the opera, it was also necessary for Britten and his supporters to raise £12,000 to launch the non-profit-making company. John Christie, Glyndebourne's inspirational, eccentric owner, was snooty about the brilliant new opera, advising old friends in the audience that this really wasn't their sort of thing. Neither was homosexuality; according to Crozier's obituary in *The Times,* Christie had walked into the composer's bedroom without knocking and caught Britten and Pears, once again cast as the central character, in a compromising situation. *Albert Herring* was dedicated, with a pinch of mischief, to novelist E.M. Forster, who wrote how he wanted to love 'a strong young man of the lower classes and be loved by him and even hurt by him'. It was also to be Britten's last Glyndebourne commission.

Peter Pears recorded the title role for Decca in 1964 (London 421 849–2) by which time he was too old to play Albert on the stage. The recording was conducted by Britten in a classic John Culshaw production, and reveals beyond doubt the homosexual subtext. Of course, in 1947, it was out of the question for Britten and Crozier's Albert to admit in the last act that he had spent the night with another man. Britten and Pears were already sailing dangerously close to the wind by living so openly together as a homosexual couple, and were risking prosecution, public humiliation and imprisonment. Instead, Albert's true fate on that wonderful, dangerous and liberating evening is signalled quite clearly to those in the audience who understood such things, while the rest might simply believe that Albert just got drunk and spent the night under the stars somewhere with a willing country girl, of which there was evidently an inexhaustible supply in fallen Loxford.

Our first glimpse of Albert shows him to be unusually strong. He enters, carrying a heavy bag of turnips, which even impresses Sid, his young heterosexual counterpart.

> 'HOW DO YOU CARRY A WEIGHT LIKE THAT ALONE?
> COR! MUST BE TWENTY STONE OR MORE!'

Sid is mad about girls and his latest, Nancy, in particular. He teases Albert for being too tied to his mother's apron strings. He's missing all the fun that a lad should enjoy, girls and sex in particular. Albert is embarrassed and carries on his work in the shop. Privately, Albert knows only too well that he is missing out on things. As Budd, the policeman, has already observed, 'He never kicks up rough as most boys do.' Albert knows that the girls don't take him seriously anyway.

> 'GIRLS DON'T CARE FOR CHAPS LIKE ME.
> I'M TOO SHY . . . I LOSE MY NERVE AND FLY.'

There's something wrong, something different about him, but he's not exactly sure what it is.

At his coronation, Albert's lemonade is spiked with spirits by Sid for a joke. The King of the May drinks it to music with echoes of *Tristan und Isolde,* a story encompassing unfulfilled passions, a love potion, forbidden sex and death. And when he returns home, a little drunk and with twenty-five gold sovereigns in his pocket (a small fortune in 1900), he knows that decisions have to be made about his life.

Before looking in more detail at what happens to Albert, when that fateful decision is made, what was life like for homosexuals in 1947? First there was fear of discovery, fear of being exposed to friends, family and the public as being queer. The dual threats of blackmail and prosecution were frighteningly real, and reverberations of the Oscar Wilde scandal, after which many homosexuals fled the country, hoping for a more tolerant life in exile, were still present half a century later. Nevertheless, a homosexual subculture, with its own territories and unwritten codes of conduct, flourished in the cities, and wartime, with its daily dangers, had made many homosexuals bolder. Bars, clubs and saunas where homosexuals were welcome existed in the cities, such as the Artists and Battledress Club in Soho, known as the 'A & B'. Many were more bohemian than exclusively gay, and apart from an occasional raid, were left to their own devices by the police.

Homosexual street culture was another matter. 'Cottaging', picking up men in public toilets, was cheap, easy and cut through the class barriers sometimes imposed by the bars and clubs. It could also be anonymous and transitory, attracting both married homosexuals and those who wanted, or needed, to lead a double life. Sex might occur in the toilets themselves, or, once the contact had been made, in more salubrious surroundings elsewhere. (One of Britten's future librettists, William Plomer, was arrested for trying to pick up a sailor at a London railway station.)

If public toilets were dimly lit by gas or electricity at night, the streets outside during the war were dark, with strict blackout regulations in force. This meant that cruising, at best by moonlight but more often in total darkness, needed its own pragmatic codes. These included the rattling of keys to indicate one's presence and attract the curious, and that special gift to the habitual cruiser, the Swan Vesta match, which can be struck against any rough surface to provide brief illumination. Swan Vestas need not, therefore, be carried in their match box (open the box upside down in the dark and you lose the lot!), and the manner in which they are struck can send a message to whoever is watching. A wall, the leather sole of a shoe, a flick of the thumbnail, or, for the truly rough at heart, a front tooth would do. Then once lit, the Swan Vesta could be used to light a cigarette or two, with the hands of the stranger cupped around the flickering light, making physical contact and allowing each man to see what the other looked like. Swan Vestas were essential and fabled equipment for the nocturnal cruiser.

Then there was a whole street culture connected with whistles. Today, the wolf-whistle, generally, but not exclusively, a male response to a passing female, remains the best known. But in the forties, other less intrusive whistles existed to attract attention. Like the jingling keys and Swan Vestas, these had their uses when cruising after dark, both to make contact with other men and to signal approaching danger. An elaborate range of whistled signals was available and widely understood in the gay subculture of the period, which is ironic since the myth that boys who couldn't whistle were 'sissies' or 'nancy boys' still had wide currency. This ludicrous belief was, in fact, the opposite of the truth. Streetwise homosexuals were mostly expert whistlers. That the police, the predatory enemy of cottagers and cruisers, should also rely on a whistle, this time of the metal variety, as their chief means of attracting attention, adds an additional twist to this long established subculture.

Whistles, Swan Vestas and even jingling in the dark, in the form of the grocer's shop bell, play important roles in *Albert Herring*. Each is used by Britten and Crozier to signal to those in the audience able to understand their significance that, beyond all doubt, Albert is homosexual. In the second scene of Act Two, Albert arrives home tipsy from his coronation. We're told in the stage directions that dusk has fallen and the only light comes from the street-lamp outside. Albert, half on the street and half in the shop, plays with the door as he sings so that the shop bell rings again and again, pointedly realized in Britten's recording, and signalling his presence to all within earshot. Then he enters the shop and calls for his mother, describing himself as 'Your sugar-plum of a prodigal son . . .' He searches for matches to light the gas and sings to the glory of Swan Vestas.

'SWAN VESTAS! SWAN VESTAS . . . ? OPEN
YOUR MOUTH, SHUT YOUR EYES, STRIKE THE MATCH FOR A NICE SURPRISE . . .'

All very camp, and the sexual innuendo is not intended to be missed by those in the know. The small gas explosion that follows is a gentle reminder that playing games with matches, like cruising at night, can also be dangerous. Albert then sings about the splendid and exotic party food which must have made mouths water in austere, food-rationed 1947, when the first post-war shipload of bananas would become the lead story on the national news.

But Albert is confused about Nancy, Sid's lass. He wonders why she blushed and stammered and caught his eye? We, of course, know the reason. She feels guilty about the spiked drink and has a friendly, sister-under-the-skin concern for Albert. He is tempted to misinterpret her behaviour as sexual attraction, but a moment's reflection rules this out, remembering that 'girls don't care for chaps like me . . . I lose my nerve and fly.' Whatever it is that girls have to offer is not, in truth, meant for boys like him.

Then Sid's whistle to Nancy is heard outside and, with Albert, we eavesdrop on the young lovers meeting in the street. They decide to have a drink, then go up to the Common to make love. Albert is left alone once more, with Sid's advice that 'Heaven helps those who help themselves' still ringing in his ears. This is the turning point of the drama, which is now poised between comedy and tragedy, action and inaction.

> 'NANCY PITIES ME — SID LAUGHS — OTHERS
> SNIGGER AT MY SIMPLICITY — OFFER ME BUNS
> TO STAY IN MY CAGE — PARADE
> ME AROUND AS THEIR WHITEHEADED BOY —
> ALBERT THE GOOD! ALBERT WHO SHOULD —
> WHO HASN'T AND WOULDN'T IF HE COULD!
> ALBERT THE MEEK! ALBERT THE SHEEP!'

Here is a boy longing to break free of the closet, sick of being patronized, petted and mocked for his blond prettiness. But he is still frightened of making a decision. He'll break one of his many taboos and gamble his future on the toss of one of his newly acquired gold sovereigns. It falls Heads for going into the night! Albert's excitement and fear is compounded by the sound of a man whistling in the dark street outside. This is emphatically *not* Sid. We know that Sid and Nancy have left for a drink and the Common sometime before. This is another man, but whistling for who? The Decca recording is especially revealing at this point. Peter Pears, as Albert, whistles back rather shyly, gets everything he needs for the night's adventure, then whistles again before leaving the shop. This second whistle quotes a snatch of the shepherd's horn call from Beethoven's Sixth Symphony. Britten and Pears are dropping us the vital clue that, with luck, Albert's deliverance, and the ultimate source of his thanksgiving, will be found that night in the arms of a local shepherd lad.

In Act Three, Albert's disappearance has turned the world of Loxford upside down. The manhunt, with echoes of *Peter Grimes,* is handled with brilliant energy and fun by Crozier and Britten, and manages to sustain that balance between comedy and tragedy so marvellously established in the previous Act. Albert's coronation wreath, that symbol of his former virgin innocence, has been found crushed by a cart 'on the road to Campsey Ash', suggesting that his deflowering has indeed been a country rather than town affair, and that Albert had excellent reason to whistle the shepherd's horn call. Just in case anyone still doubts Albert's homosexuality, 'Campsey Ash' is an obvious anagram of 'Yes! A.H.'s Camp!' Albert's account of the 'wild explosion' of his night's adventures to the outraged worthies of Loxford is graphic enough about the early and drunken part of the evening, but tactfully stops short of the rest.

Having asserted his new independence to both the community and to his wretched mother, our hero is left in his new Eden with the free-spirited children, Emmie, Cis and Harry, and the young lovers, Sid and Nancy. No need for the kids to pinch apples any more. Albert's 'Have a nice peach?' (delivered with a grotesque and wanton leer by Pears in the recording) promises joyful indulgence to the liberated minority in his fallen Paradise.

... 'Weep ... 'Weep ...

THE LITTLE SWEEP:
LIBRETTIST ERIC CROZIER, FIRST
PERFORMANCE ON 14TH JUNE 1949
AT ALDEBURGH

THE GOLDEN VANITY:
TEXT BY COLIN GRAHAM, FIRST
PERFORMANCE BY THE VIENNA BOYS'
CHOIR ON 3RD JUNE 1967 AT
THE MALTINGS, SNAPE

CHILDREN'S CRUSADE':
POEM BY BRECHT, TRANSLATED BY
HANS KELLER, FIRST PERFORMANCE
BY THE WANDSWORTH SCHOOL
CHOIR AND ORCHESTRA ON 19TH
MAY 1969 AT WESTMINSTER
CATHEDRAL

Different genres they may be, but these three works, spanning twenty years, demonstrate Britten's desire to protest publicly against the abuse of children as well as to show his dramatic skills in the theatre and on the concert platform. Sam, the little sweep, is forced to endure the dangers and discomforts of climbing the chimneys of the rich. The cabin boy of the *Golden Vanity* strips off (as Sam also must to climb and to be scrubbed clean by the other children) to sink the pirate ship and is then betrayed by Captain, Bosun and crew and left to drown. Then, in the Brecht setting, fifty-five Polish refugee children seek peace and sanctuary in war-torn Europe only to disappear mysteriously, leaving only their starving dog with a scrawled message hanging around its neck. There may be hope for Sam, and the drowned cabin boy can, at least, come back to life and march off the concert platform with the other boys, but Brecht's children, after many adventures, take leave of this world with their individual fates unrecorded.

The Golden Vanity, described by Britten as a vaudeville, was written for the Vienna Boys' Choir, who wanted an all-male story so they wouldn't have to dress up as women. Copland had already set the same ballad as one of his 'Old American Songs', but Britten's version, with words by director Colin Graham, is acted out in a costumed platform production, complete with on-stage sound effects of splashing water and a comical cannon shot, recalling the abortive battle scene in *Billy Budd*. Behind this playground fun, a deadly serious tragedy is enacted. The cabin boy, who saves the lives of his entire crew by swimming to the pirate ship and drilling a hole beneath its waterline, is left to drown so his shipmates, the Bosun and Captain don't have to pay what they owe. His pathetic cries for help go unheeded until it is too late.

Part of the fun of *The Golden Vanity* is in boys playing adults without ever forgetting they are youngsters, so in time-honoured role-playing tradition, the drowned cabin boy can spring back to life at the end of the story and rejoin his mates. The *Children's Crusade* reverses this situation. The children, boys and girls in the story this time, although sung entirely by boys, are forced by the ravages of war to assume the responsibilities of adults to try and survive. But throughout, we are painfully aware that they are simply children. A handful of the fifty-five children emerge briefly as characters, including a little Jew, a boy from the Nazi legation and a drummer boy. In one of the glimpses of their adventures, we learn that a pair of lovers, living like grown-ups, are just twelve and fifteen years old. Nine soloists from the choir assume these roles from the story, which is told entirely in the past tense. Although the result is intensely dramatic, with an unforgettable part for the barking dog, this 'Ballad for Children's Voices and Orchestra' is not dramatized like an operatic libretto. The result is a curious hybrid, part choral ballad, part mini-oratorio, which is crucially dependent on all the words being crystal clear and comprehensible to make its effect. Unlike an acted out drama where we can follow most of the story from what we see, the *Children's Crusade,* whose nineteen minutes are packed with enough narrative for a full-length opera, demands a mastery of diction and powers of dramatic communication from its young performers. Written to celebrate fifty years of the Save the Children Fund, and strikingly bleak and nihilistic in outlook, *Children's Crusade* is a major work and far more successful than the pacifist opera, *Owen Wingrave,* that followed it.

At the age of five, Britten had played the part of Tom the Sweep. *The Water Babies* of Charles Kingsley had been published in 1863, so this strange and sensual book, with its social conscience mingled with a reverence for the natural world, was almost contemporary literature to Britten's parents. Crozier and Britten had discussed the possibility of collaborating on an opera for children as early as 1947. Arthur Ransome's *Swallows and Amazons* was mentioned, but Britten, remembering Blake's *Songs of Innocence and Experience,* made a connection between his own memories of playing Tom and the fate of abused, young chimney sweepers, who cried

> . . . 'WEEP . . . 'WEEP . . . . 'WEEP
> IN NOTES OF WOE . . .'

After the success of the first Aldeburgh Festival in 1948, the idea of a children's opera was raised again, with Crozier as librettist, and a loose adaptation of part of *The Water Babies* was decided upon. The operatic version was set in nearby Iken Hall in 1810. A nine-year-old sweep boy, now called Sam, gets stuck up a chimney, is rescued by upper-class children, bathed, hidden in a toy cupboard and smuggled to freedom in a trunk. Lots of action is combined with swift narrative. Children are good. Adults, apart from Rowan the nursery-maid, are bad or downright evil. As with the cantata *Saint Nicolas* of 1948 (another Crozier collaboration), the audience was required to sing certain numbers, but unlike the cantata, with its two familiar hymns, *The Little Sweep*'s three audience songs are original and more difficult to perform. The advantage of audience songs lies in the way all those present have the opportunity to participate directly in the drama. The risk is that some audiences make such a poor showing that they end up alienated from the proceedings by their sense of failure. The next time Britten used this device, in *Noye's Fludde,* he wisely resorted once again to Anglican hymns, to stunning effect. In *The Little Sweep,* there is a good case for absorbing the audience songs into the production, using extra resources as necessary, and fully dramatizing their performance.

This 'rescue opera' has some things in common with *Albert Herring,* with its liberation of a young man who uses the gift of unexpected money ('three shining half-crowns' in Sam's case) to build a new life. But, *The Little Sweep,* for all its narrative power, lacks complex, fully rounded characters. Crozier's libretto looks like a first draft, although it surely wasn't, and has nothing like the imaginative energy or technical address of *Albert Herring.* If Crozier's work displays haste, it isn't at all surprising. Britten was preoccupied with the completion of the *Spring Symphony,* while Crozier and E.M. Forster were already at work on *Billy Budd*. In *The Little Sweep,* the dialogue that links the numbers is functional rather than sharply focused, and nothing much distinguishes the individual personalities of the children. Nevertheless, some lines are memorable and sinister, with hints of sexual abuse lurking beneath the surface:

'CHIMBLEY-SWEEPERS MUST 'AVE BOYS
SAME AS POACHERS MUST 'AVE FERRETS.'

'CHOOSE 'EM NIMBLE, SPRY AND THIN —
THAT'S THE CHAP FOR CHIMBLEY-SWEEPING!
EASY, TOO, FOR BREAKING IN,
BAR A BIT OF TEARS AND WEEPING.'

Sam's body, clothed and unclothed, whether clean and white or covered with soot, achieves iconographic status. His stripping by Black Bob and Clem is a humiliating fall from grace.

'NOW, LITTLE WHITE BOY!
SHIVER-WITH-FRIGHT BOY!
SCARED-IN-THE-NIGHT BOY!
TIME FOR YOUR CLIMB!

CLOTHES OFF, MY BRIGHT BOY!
DON'T KICK AND FIGHT, BOY!
OH! SO YOU'D BITE, BOY — ?
TIME FOR YOUR CLIMB!'

Sam is, in effect, violated by the two men, who even require the wretched, protesting child to kiss them before he climbs. Conversely, after he is rescued from the chimney by the children, his soot-black body is bathed and scrubbed white again, like a resurrected soul washed clean. But if Sam, unlike Grimes's apprentices, the missing boy in *Curlew River,* Miles in *The Turn of the Screw* and the fifty-five refugee children in *Children's Crusade,* lives to tell the tale, the horrid housekeeper, Miss Baggott, reminds us that there are 'four more chimneys on this floor' to be swept and heaven knows how many elsewhere in this rich household, and we know that if it isn't Sam who will have to climb them, some other poor lad will. A soul saved may be a battle won, but the war against child abuse rages on.

ERIC CROZIER AND E.M. FORSTER, 1949

'I want to love a strong young man of the lower classes and be loved by him and even hurt by him.'

The angel must hang

BILLY BUDD:

LIBRETTISTS E.M. FORSTER AND ERIC CROZIER, FIRST PERFORMANCE OF FOUR-ACT VERSION ON 1ST DECEMBER 1951 AT COVENT GARDEN, FIRST PERFORMANCE OF REVISED TWO-ACT VERSION ON 13TH NOVEMBER 1961 ON BBC RADIO THIRD PROGRAMME

'I want to love a strong young man of the lower classes and be loved by him and even hurt by him.' Not the wish of Britten, of course, for whom a boy from any social background might be the object of affection, but the words of E.M. Forster, a homosexual of very different persuasions. Forster would have loved to have been the anonymous whistler outside Albert Herring's grocery, although he would have whisked the young man off to Campsey Ash in a taxi, not a cart, while Britten might have been content to play hide and seek or Happy Families in the shop with the children. Therein lies the conflict of personality that prevented Britten's next opera, *Billy Budd*, from achieving its full dramatic potential.

Forster had already triggered Britten's return from America with his essay on Crabbe and Suffolk. The understated homoerotic subtexts of his published novels and some of his short stories (*Maurice* – unusually, a novel about a successful gay relationship – was not published until after Forster's death), to say nothing of his international reputation, made Forster an interesting choice as librettist. Similarly, Herman Melville's novel, *Billy Budd, Foretopman,* begun in 1886, was not published until 1924, thirty-three years after the author's death, the very year that Forster's *A Passage to India* was published. Eric Crozier was once again called upon, this time to assist Forster, who was inexperienced in theatre writing. The homoerotic ambience of sailors at sea, and the sexual ambiguities of Melville's story excited Forster, who also had an intuitive response to music, as demonstrated in the famous Beethoven's Fifth Symphony passage in *Howard's End* and in his essay 'Not Listening to Music' (*The Listener*, 19th January 1939):

'. . . *The slow start of Beethoven's Seventh Symphony invokes a grey-green tapestry of hunting scenes, and the slow movement of his Fourth Piano Concerto (the dialogue between piano and orchestra) reminds me of the dialogue between Orpheus and the Furies in Gluck. The climax of the first movement of the Apassionata (the 'piu allegro') seems to me sexual, although I can detect no sex in the Kreutzer, nor have I come across anyone who could, except Tolstoy.'*

Next to Auden, Forster was the most brilliant literary talent among Britten's collaborators. Although not as dominating as the poet, he could be just as challenging and outspoken. The way he translated what he heard into visual and dramatic images, rather than analyse music in purely musical terms, was also to bring him into conflict with Britten.

Melville's novel was inspired by the fate of Elisha Small, a sailor aboard the US brig *Somers* who was hanged in November 1842. Rumours of conspiracy to mutiny were brought to the Captain's notice by the ship's Lieutenant and, although the evidence against him was flimsy, the unfortunate Small was hanged to set an example to the rest of the crew. He made an astonishingly brave show of it. The Captain asked Small, who had become a handsome sailor by the time he reached Melville's novella, if he would forgive him for what he felt he had to do. Small replied: 'Yes, sir, and I honour you for it; God bless that flag!'

In transferring the action of the novel from an American to a British ship, Forster and Crozier created a very different world for the new opera. Humphrey Carpenter points out shrewdly that life on the *Indomitable* resembles the closed world of the English boarding school, with its rigid hierarchy of prefects, fags, sneaks, dreary routines and strict rules. The ship is also, of course, an entirely male world in which the sexuality of its crew has to be sublimated one way or another, and the addition of rum to buggery and the lash sometimes seems all that divides the sailors from the schoolboys.

The opera starts and ends with Captain Vere as an old man. He is still haunted by the events of the summer of 1797 when the beautiful sailor he hanged changed his life for ever.

'BUT HE HAS SAVED ME, AND BLESSED ME, AND THE LOVE THAT PASSETH UNDERSTANDING HAS COME TO ME. I WAS LOST ON THE INFINITE SEA, BUT I'VE SIGHTED A SAIL IN THE STORM, THE FAR SHINING SAIL, AND I'M CONTENT. I'VE SEEN WHERE SHE'S BOUND FOR. THERE'S A LAND WHERE SHE'LL ANCHOR FOR EVER.'

The religious tone of Vere's musings and the vision of life after death, with which Billy Budd's passion has blessed him, are either profoundly touching or grossly maudlin, depending on how one reacts to the central story. Billy Budd is one of three sailors pressed to join the crew of the *Indomitable* from another ship, the *Rights o' Man*. His farewell to his previous ship, with its provocative and revolutionary name, is misunderstood by the officers, evidently a very dim lot not to realize it was the ship he was referring to and not Tom Paine's political book. Billy accepts being pressed into service with positive enthusiasm, and like the equally unfortunate Tom Bowling of Dibdin's memorable song, soon becomes 'the darling of our crew'. The bad news is that the Master-at-Arms, John Claggart, confronted by such dazzling beauty and virtue, feels compelled to destroy Billy by foul means. In a melodramatic monologue, reminding one of Iago's Credo in Verdi's *Otello*, Claggart tries to explain himself, with perverted echoes of the King James Bible:

'WOULD THAT I LIVED IN MY OWN WORLD ALWAYS, IN THAT DEPRAVITY TO WHICH I WAS BORN. THERE I FOUND PEACE OF A SORT, THERE I ESTABLISHED AN ORDER SUCH AS REIGNS IN HELL. BUT ALAS, ALAS! THE LIGHT SHINES IN THE DARKNESS, AND THE DARKNESS COMPREHENDS IT AND SUFFERS.'

But what is 'that depravity'? Presumably, if one is to try and define it literally, Claggart is referring to his homosexual nature, about which he has a totally negative attitude. But like so much in this opera, literal facts are obscured by swirls of sea mist and occasional banks of thick fog. Forster had no doubt what this monologue of Claggart's was all about:

'I WANT PASSION — LOVE CONSTRICTED, PERVERTED, POISONED, BUT NEVER THE LESS FLOWING DOWN ITS AGONISING CHANNEL; A SEXUAL DISCHARGE GONE EVIL.'

Unfortunately, what Forster heard in the music was 'soggy depression' and 'growling remorse', and he had no hesitation in telling the sensitive Britten what he thought. It's a tragedy that Britten didn't listen to the advice of his librettist, for the Claggart that emerged has neither the dramatic stature or psychological complexity of Peter Grimes, but is instead another one-dimensional villain like Black Bob in *The Little Sweep,* only this time writ large. Britten seems to view him as a man so disgusted by his sexuality that he exacts cruel revenge on those who arouse his desire. If the musical response that Forster wanted was quite different from the composer's intention (and one feels, rightly or wrongly, that Britten could write music for any situation if he turned his mind to it), one might add that the librettists made a dreadful error in writing this crass monologue in the first place, even if such a passage had been specifically requested by the composer. As should have been clear from Verdi's error of judgement in *Otello,* it is far better that an audience experiences the complexity of a character from his actions than that everything is expressed crudely in a monologue, like a villain in a pantomime.

Captain Vere is even more of a puzzle than Claggart. He tries to salve his conscience at his participation in a judicial murder by imagining that, in some mystical way, Billy Budd has shown him a vision of salvation. A thoughtful man with a classical education, whose name suggests honesty and truth, he reminds one of a weak and irresolute headmaster who'll give in to any pressure to steer a steady course. He knew he could have saved Billy, but he lacked the guts to do so. He allowed himself to become Claggart's instrument of destruction, suggesting that he too was suppressing a deep desire for some sort of relationship with the beautiful young sailor, a private conflict with which Britten, with his attraction to young boys, was only too painfully aware.

The one scene that would have clarified this is missing from the opera. After the verdict of the court has been delivered, Vere has a private meeting with Billy to tell him of the outcome. What happens between Billy and Vere in the privacy of the Captain's cabin is of vital significance to the plot. Indeed, it is this very confrontation that changes Vere's life for ever and is the cause of him telling us his story all these years later. Melville tells us that, 'Beyond the communication of the sentence, what took place at this interview was never known.' But it is certain that Vere himself knew perfectly well what took place and exactly what was said, and in the opera, as a direct result of the framing device, Billy's story is told to us by Vere himself. There is a case for Melville shrouding the interview in mystery, although he didn't have to, but there is none with the elderly Vere telling us everything. In spite of this, Britten writes an orchestral interlude consisting of thirty-four chords instead of dramatizing the scene. These certainly make a profound impression when first encountered in the theatre, although repeated hearings blunt their impact, and the feeling that one has somehow been cheated out of so crucial a moment in the drama undermines the credibility of the entire opera.

So what did the two men actually say to each other? It's a safe bet that Vere tells Billy that the court has found him guilty and that he must hang in the morning. He's very sorry about this, but there's not much he can do. The court has made its decision. Billy knows that Vere was the only witness to Claggart's death. There were various ways in which the Captain could have presented the facts without perjuring himself and which might have saved the young man's life. Even at that late stage, the Captain has the authority to commute the sentence or instigate an appeal, but he doesn't. Like a good angel, Billy understands the older man's weakness, forgives him and blesses him. We know that Billy is a foundling. Had Vere given thought to adopting him? Billy is one of those men that everyone loves. There is, for example, a touching relationship between Dansker, an old salt battered by experience but retaining a heart of gold, and Billy, who he calls 'Beauty' and 'Baby'.

In contrast, there is also the curious and excellent sub-plot concerning the unnamed Novice. He is lashed for a minor offence and returns from his punishment full of shame, as though he has been the victim of rape. Now a broken lad (a very young tenor is essential casting) and under Claggart's control, he betrays Billy, who, like the rest of the crew, he loves, with planted French gold.

All this is fine and excellent drama, and no one aboard is in any doubt that at the opera's tragic climax, an angel is hanged when Billy fearlessly drops into the abyss. His cry of 'Starry Vere, God bless you!' echoes the courage of the real life Elisha Small. Edward Fairfax Vere's nickname comes oddly, and not entirely comprehensibly, from lines in Andrew Marvell's poem, 'Upon Appleton House':

'THIS 'TIS TO HAVE BEEN FROM THE FIRST
IN A DOMESTIC HEAVEN NURSED,
UNDER THE DISCIPLINE SEVERE
OF FAIRFAX AND THE STARRY VERE.'

Presumably, the sailors have adopted the nickname without a clue of its origin. There is another resonant couplet in 'Upon Appleton House':

'WHENCE, FOR SOME UNIVERSAL GOOD,
THE PRIEST SHALL CUT THE SACRED BUD.'

Vere believes he is sacrificing Budd for the universal good of the ship, as though Abraham has chosen to ignore the ram caught in the thicket and has slaughtered his own son. But whether Billy's blessing is the fulfilment of the unwritten scene of the previous night, sadly, we can only guess.

What another composer, gay or otherwise, might have made of the Forster and Crozier libretto, and how it might have been developed, is a tantalizing thought. Michael Tippett visited Britten while *Billy Budd* was being written and had to point out that the line 'Clear the deck of seamen!' was, perhaps, a little unfortunate. It is hard to think of Tippett fudging the homoerotic and male bonding themes as blatantly as Britten does. Britten had neither the confidence nor the sexual maturity to write the fateful scene, even though the credibility of the opera depends so heavily upon it. That the meeting between Billy and Vere arouses so much speculation underlines the feebleness of the decision to fob us off with music alone, however initially impressive. The result is a mortal wound from which this opera, beautiful, gripping and memorable as it is, will never recover.

Mean queen

GLORIANA:

LIBRETTIST WILLIAM PLOMER, FIRST PERFORMED ON 8TH JUNE 1953
AT THE ROYAL OPERA HOUSE, COVENT GARDEN

'A vein, undeniably, of homophobia, not very visible or audible, but certainly there, pulsing disagreeably away.' Thus Donald Mitchell describes the atmosphere surrounding the world première of *Gloriana,* specially commissioned in honour of the Coronation of Queen Elizabeth II and performed in her presence. The notion that British theatres and opera houses are peopled by homosexuals still persists to this day in some quarters, and is as false now as it was in 1953. Nevertheless, Britten's high profile, prestigious commissions and breathtaking productivity were the source of irritation and envy amongst lesser artists. Misguidedly, the recently knighted Sir William Walton was grumbling about Britten getting the Covent Garden commission in the first place: 'There are enough buggers in the place already, it's time it was stopped . . . Everyone is queer and I'm just normal, so my music will never succeed.'

According to Sir Michael Tippett, rumours that there was a homosexual conspiracy in the musical world, engineered by Britten and Pears, were fostered by Elizabeth Lutyens, Constant Lambert and Alan Rawsthorne, among others, as though Britten were getting preferential treatment when it came to prestigious commissions, from closet homosexuals in powerful positions of authority. In fact, there were rich opportunities in the fifties for the commissioning and performing of new British operas by a wide variety of composers. At Sadler's Wells alone, Vilem Tausky premièred Sir Lennox Berkeley's *Nelson* and *The Dinner Engagement,* Thea Musgrave's *The Abbot of Drimock* and Malcolm Williamson's *Our Man in Havana* and *The Violins of St Jacques.* However, in 1953, many establishment knives were out long before the curtain rose on that June evening, with its grand society audience. It is curious to note that the Britten bashing that occurred in much of the press was focused on an opera that did not have

WILLIAM PLOMER, 1960

Britten's latest librettist was William Plomer, novelist and poet, born in South Africa, educated at Rugby, sometime African farmer and trader, world traveller and homosexual.

an obvious homosexual subtext, as though the critics welcomed the chance to hold up their hands innocently and say, 'Homophobic? Us?'

Antagonism towards homosexuals was not confined to the musical world. In 1952, the defection of Burgess and Maclean to Moscow, which fuelled the prejudice that homosexuals were treacherous by nature, determined the Home Secretary, Sir David Maxwell-Fyfe, to instigate 'a new drive against male vice' once the dust on the spy scandal had settled. Consequently, between 1953 and 1956, 480 adult males in England and Wales were convicted of sexual offences with consenting adults in private. Scotland Yard detectives interviewed many suspected homosexuals, including, in December 1953, just months after the première of *Gloriana,* Britten himself. (The evidence for this exists only in a memo from Percy Elland, then the editor of the *Evening Standard*, to Lord Beaverbrook, his proprietor.) While no action was taken against the composer, huge publicity attended the arrest and trial of Lord Montagu of Beaulieu, Michael Pitt-Rivers and Peter Wildeblood for homosexual offences between consenting adults committed in 1952. All three were imprisoned after their trial in 1954. In an atmosphere of such homophobic hysteria, the Coronation opera must have seemed safe ground after *Billy Budd*, with its steamy story of sailors at sea.

The new opera itself concerned an ageing woman in a position of absolute power, who frequently refers to herself as 'Prince' rather than 'Queen', and who places duty and service to country ahead of personal and private considerations. What, in view of the public celebrations heralding the new Elizabethan age, could be more apt? Britten's opera is full of public pageantry and celebration of the monarch. There's a splendid masque in Norwich, a jousting tournament (off stage), and much dancing at court. Indeed, the extended and elaborate ensembles and choruses are just some of the many memorable features of this rich and spectacular work. But it is also far more than a triumphal, nationalistic, occasional piece. The two central characters of Elizabeth and Essex are finely conceived, each with its contradictions and frailties, each making a fascinating, personal journey towards self-knowledge in the course of the narrative. If only the same sound dramatic principles had been applied to

Billy Budd. And time has been kind to the Coronation opera. In spite of its initial vicious critical reception which had little to do with its musical and dramatic power, *Gloriana* is proving a durable and effective addition to the international stage, with memorable productions, notably by Opera North, and an outstanding recording conducted by Sir Charles Mackerras (Argo 440 213–40).

Britten's latest librettist was William Plomer, novelist and poet, born in South Africa, educated at Rugby, sometime African farmer and trader, world traveller and homosexual. He published his autobiography, *Double Lives*, in 1943 at the age of forty and was turning fifty at the time of his first collaboration with Britten. Unlike Duncan and Crozier, he worked at a distance from the composer, declining to use the telephone and communicating instead by letter, like a librettist of a bygone age. He used Lytton Strachey's *Elizabeth and Essex* (1928) and J.E. Neale's biography *Queen Elizabeth* (1934) as his prime sources. To provide a period flavour, Plomer sprinkled his work with archaicisms, dusting down 'malapert', 'plainings', 'complot' and, probably for the first time, and hopefully the last on the British stage, 'slubberdegullion'. He just about gets away with it. There are times when a naughty schoolboy seems to be meddling with 'Merrie England' ('Willy Wet-leg, you won't burn!' . . . 'Slattern, I'll have your blood!'); and an innocent looking line like 'What rabble is this?' was always bound to invite a ribald audience response. But overall, Plomer's work is solid and practical, rather than inspired or original. He manages to balance the public and private aspects of the plot with skill, so that even during scenes of public spectacle, the personal turmoil beneath the surface is still seen to be simmering away. Similarly, and importantly, in the private scenes between Elizabeth and Essex, the world outside, with ears listening and powerful forces (centred on the indestructible Sir Robert Cecil, manipulating and biding his time), is always only an arras away.

Britten's head-count of librettists was growing. Auden, Duncan and Forster were out for good, and loyal, trusty Crozier, by now the veteran of many projects, was on his way. Even while Plomer was at work on the Coronation commission, Myfanwy Piper (wife of artist John Piper) was

starting work on Britten's next opera, *The Turn of The Screw*. That Duncan
and Forster should be dropped is understandable and the composer's need
to maintain his independence as an artist and a private individual from the
dominating, not to say abusive, Auden was sad but probably essential. But
Crozier's ultimate rejection, after such sterling service, was insulting and
hurtful. If, shadowing Elizabeth in the opera, Britten felt that artistic affairs
took precedence over personal matters, there was no need for him to play
the mean queen to the hilt. On the other hand, in addition to many other
commissions, to say nothing of overseeing the now annual Aldeburgh
Festival, he had been writing a new opera every eighteen months or so
since *Peter Grimes*. This truly astonishing, hyperactive achievement was
bound to take its toll and unfortunately this manifested itself in the
personal rejection of those deemed expendable. But it was also necessary to
set one project going while another was being completed, and this
required a small team of librettists to keep up with the pace. And there
never was an available pool of experienced librettists to choose from in the
first place. Britten, with his rapid, ruthless operatic production line, was, in
effect, master-minding a new British industry.

The crucial role of Essex was written, once again, for Peter Pears, but he
was less than happy at being cast as what he perceived as a conventional
lover. 'I'm not sure, but I think somebody else should have done it rather
than me.' This is a puzzling reaction, perhaps concealing more than it
reveals. It must be obvious at a glance that Essex is no ordinary tenor role.
And lover? What does this supposed love for Elizabeth really consist of? He
is half her age, which does not in itself militate against sexual desire, but his
primary and eventually destructive passion is personal ambition. He wants
authority from 'his Prince' to go to Ireland to defeat the rebel Tyrone. After
that, he feels that his power and his triumphant army will return to England
to claim the throne. For all her fascination and affection for 'Robin' (a
diminutive of 'Robert'), she sees through him and by sending him, after a
calculated delay, on the disastrous Irish mission, she provides him, coolly
and deliberately, with the means of his own destruction. Central to the
credibility of their relationship are the two lute songs, 'Quick music is best'
and 'Happy were he . . .' which display Essex as the true original poet, able

to extemporize in words and music to exquisite effect. Who would not love such a man, whatever his faults? Yet this is also the same person who, behind her back, can describe Elizabeth as '. . . crooked as her carcass!' and can plot, shamelessly, to seize the throne for himself. In the end, given the custom of the age, he deserves nothing less than the axe. Given such a splendidly conceived role to play, with music to match, why was Pears so diffident about his casting? Was it more to do with the private world of composer and singer? Was Britten, the powerful prime mover, sounding a warning to his lover that his personal loyalty was under scrutiny, and if needs be, Pears would be cut out of his life? The impression one gets is that while Britten remained obsessed by a series of boys, Pears was sexually active elsewhere. But there are too many pieces missing from the jigsaw, at present, to be sure. Nevertheless, Robert Devereux, Earl of Essex, cut too near the bone for comfort.

Elizabeth, for her part, for all her capacity to survive, can also play the bitch. She humiliates Lady Essex in the most cruel fashion by stealing her dress and wearing the ill-fitting garment to grotesque effect at the Whitehall Ball. She also uses the advice of her 'elf', Cecil, to procrastinate, to find the perfect moment, to dispatch the dangerous Essex to his doom. She may justify her actions by believing that they are in the best interests of her people and her country, but when needs must, she proves a deadly and venomous creature.

Throughout the score, Britten is at his least inhibited, knowing that this time he is not concealing skeletons in his own cupboard. He transfuses Plomer's solid libretto with dazzling invention that never slips into clumsy parody or empty pastiche. Visual spectacle is coupled with two vivid and complex central roles, which challenge so splendidly the talents of the greatest actor-singers.

This queer life

THE TURN OF THE SCREW:
LIBRETTIST MYFANWY PIPER, FIRST PERFORMANCE ON 14TH SEPTEMBER 1954 AT THE FENICE IN VENICE

Within weeks of being interviewed by the Scotland Yard detectives as part of Maxwell-Fyfe's witch-hunt to root out 'male vice', Britten was working at full pressure on an opera with more than a hint of child abuse and paedophilia. He had to complete his work in a mere five months. His right arm was causing him pain and bursitis (inflammation in the right shoulder) was diagnosed, so he commenced his task by writing his score with his left hand. In spite of the unconcealed fact that he was living in partnership with another man and had been the subject of police scrutiny, he seems to have led a charmed life. Pears may have had a separate bedroom from the start, and spent considerable time apart from Britten, either staying for much of the week in London, or fulfilling concert engagements, but only the most simple-minded observers could have doubted the nature of their relationship. Whether he had the protection of powerful friends, whether the police shrugged their shoulders and thought that attempting a prosecution was more trouble than it was worth, or whether he was just plain lucky, is hard to tell. He was, in fact, at greater risk of prosecution at this stage of his life than at any other simply for sharing his life with another adult male, as the fate of hundreds of other less fortunate adult homosexuals during the next few years attests, which makes the very nature of his new opera explicitly risky.

While the heterosexual subject matter of *Gloriana* was safe enough in the context of those repressive times, that of *The Turn of The Screw* certainly was not, even though Henry James's short story of 1898, which had been dramatized for BBC radio before the war, was an established classic. Yet Britten's confidence in tackling the story of adults fighting to possess the souls and bodies of two children under such circumstances is extraordinary. It suggests that he felt immune from charges of sexual abuse from any of

L–R : BENJAMIN BRITTEN, MYFANWY PIPER, PETER PEARS AND
EDWARD PIPER AT GAGHOUSE, ALDEBURGH, 1950S

Myfanwy Piper, the mother of four children herself,
had with husband John, been part of Britten's inner
circle for some years...Here was someone intelligent
and literate whom Britten knew and trusted.

the boys that he had taken to his heart over the years simply because, whatever private fantasies he entertained, he had shown consistent self-restraint when it came to translating thought into action. All the men interviewed by Humphrey Carpenter, who were intimate with Britten as boys, tell the same story: treats, cuddles, paternal kisses, baths after tennis, on rare occasions the same bed even, but no sex. Britten must have felt, with characteristic naïvety, that he could never get into trouble for what he hadn't done. None of his boys would point a false finger.

Myfanwy Piper, the mother of four children herself, had, with husband John, been part of Britten's inner circle for some years. The composer had bounced ideas off her in the past and her unexpected new role as librettist evolved through chance and circumstance. Here was someone intelligent and literate whom Britten knew and trusted. This time, his instinct was entirely vindicated. The libretto that they fashioned together, with its sixteen scenes and a Prologue, linked by fifteen orchestral variations, is an outstanding success. Where Plomer might have written every episode with a beginning, a middle and an end, Piper cut into scenes at their crucial moments, showing us the important bit before cutting away again. Stated simply, she applied the cinematographic skills of a screenwriter. Thus, after a Prologue which sets the scene, viewing the action with a forward time shift, she cuts directly to the Governess in her coach, travelling to Bly. We don't see her getting into or out of the coach, which, one suspects, is what Plomer would have done. The fact that the opera was originally conceived as a film project, to help finance the operations of the English Opera Group, may also have affected its final theatrical structure. Anyway, its razor-sharp dramatic focus and fluid, lean cutting from one scene to the next, contributes hugely to the overall success of the opera.

That Prologue, sung on the 1955 recording by Pears (Decca 425 672–2), who also doubles as the ghost, Peter Quint, establishes that the source of the story is the Governess's own account, 'written in faded ink'. The narrative that follows is therefore partial, subjective and not necessarily to be trusted. The entire opera might be an elaborate figment of the Governess's hysterical imagination. Yet the action that follows is so vivid that one never doubts what one sees and hears. The Governess, whose name we never know and who has been asked to take charge of the two children, Miles and Flora, by their absentee Guardian, at no time tells the story in retrospect herself. Instead, the narrative is always in the time present, confronting us with the drama as it unfolds, with all its ambiguities and unanswered questions.

Do the ghosts exist? Yes. When the Governess describes the man she has seen up the tower, Mrs Grose, the housekeeper, recognizes him immediately as Peter Quint. The Governess could not have made up so precise a description of someone of whose existence she was unaware previously. She must have seen Quint. His ghost, therefore, exists in our mortal world. Similarly, the ghost of Miss Jessel, a former governess, is also real. Flora senses when she is present, even without looking in her direction. But at the start of Act Two, there's a scene between Quint and Miss Jessel which cross-fades from the ghosts to the Governess, suggesting that what we've just witnessed may indeed be a figment of the Governess's disturbed imagination. By the time we reach Act Two, Scene Seven, the Governess is so distracted that she believes she can see Miss Jessel even though Mrs Grose cannot. The fact that the housekeeper denies the presence of Miss Jessel seems to break the spell that the ghost has over Flora, as though the Governess's hysteria has become the prime source of the supernatural apparition:

'I CAN'T SEE ANYBODY,
CAN'T SEE ANYTHING,
NOBODY, NOTHING.'

As a consequence, Flora is rescued by Mrs Grose, who takes her away from Bly with all possible haste, leaving Miles to be fought over by the Governess and Quint. The screw is turning for the last time. Now it is Quint who is trying to rescue Miles from the psychosis of the woman. Disastrously, the boy is so confused about the nature of good and evil that he fails to see that Quint is the angel that could save him and that the true devil is the Governess. Choosing the woman, not the man, kills him.

Miles ('soldier') is more precisely depicted than his sister, Flora ('goddess of flowers and plants'). What we see is an extremely gifted and imaginative boy, who is expelled from his school for what is described as 'an injury to his friends'. This sounds as though it is a euphemism for some unspecified sexual transgression with other boys. Quint, who has 'made free' with him, appeals to the boy like a latter-day Oberon bewitching a fairy child:

'I AM ALL THINGS STRANGE AND BOLD,

THE RIDERLESS HORSE

SNORTING, STAMPING ON THE HARD SEA SAND,

THE HERO-HIGHWAYMAN PLUNDERING THE LAND.

I AM KING MIDAS WITH GOLD IN HIS HAND.'

'Making free' carries with it sexual suggestion as well as the liberation of the senses. Quint is not merely a wicked man who sexually abuses boys, although he makes it clear to Miss Jessel in that same opening scene of Act Two (which, remember, may be a projection of the Governess's imagination) that it isn't a woman that he needs:

'I SEEK A FRIEND —

OBEDIENT TO FOLLOW WHERE I LEAD.

SLICK AS A JUGGLER'S MATE TO CATCH

MY THOUGHT,

PROUD, CURIOUS, AGILE, HE SHALL FEED

MY MOUNTING POWER . . .'

It is the young, fresh image of the perfect boy that is at the forefront of his fantasy, and, for the time being, Miles is his prime object of desire. What Quint wants to develop in the lad is an awareness of the fullest potential of his sensual, imaginative and creative side, of which his sexuality is only one aspect. Quint is challenging the deadening orthodoxy of Christianity and middle-class English values, as represented by Mrs Grose and the unnamed Governess, which have imprisoned him. It is the conflict between libidinous free spirit ('experience' to William Blake and a creative, positive force) and the stifling dullness of little England (Blake's restrictive, negative, emotionally and creatively stunting 'innocence') that eventually suffocates the life out of Miles.

It was Britten who provided Piper with the haunting extracts from the Latin primer which were originally intended to help a young scholar learn the different meanings of 'malo'. All the child would have to say to himself would be:

'I WOULD RATHER BE

IN AN APPLE TREE

THAN A NAUGHTY BOY

IN ADVERSITY'

to have all four meanings on the tip of his tongue. For Miles, however, in a masterly dramatic stroke, the simple schoolboy lesson becomes an incantation, expressing the dilemma in which the boy finds himself. What do these adults mean? Being in an apple tree sounds fun, but in Genesis the fruit of the Tree of Knowledge was used by the Serpent to tempt Eve and precipitate the Fall of Mankind. But if a boy is also 'naughty' when not in the apple tree where can goodness possibly reside? Are we all 'bad' whether we want to be or not in 'this queer life'? It is a puzzle to which Miles can find no satisfactory answer, nor can the living adults help him in the least. Only Quint, his dead friend, seemed to have the answer. Surrender to your instincts. Live your life for all it's worth. Abandon innocence. Explore the outer reaches of experience. Taste all its fruits fearlessly.

How Britten would love to have played Quint to the full with the boys in his life. In fact, life and art did meet for a while in the person of the young David Hemmings, destined for a long and distinguished career as a screen actor, who played Miles at the Venice première. Hemmings appears to have been an unusually liberated and worldly boy of exceptional beauty and intelligence. His performance in the Decca recording is astonishing for its complete identification with Miles. His haunting by Quint at the end of Act One is chilling and fascinating by turns: 'I'm here . . . O I'm here!' sounding every inch the fallen child, unable to resist the ravishing of the senses to which he has become addicted and in which he seeks salvation. Britten's relationship with young Hemmings is examined in detail by Carpenter. It was evidently the cause of much concern to some of the other singers in the company, who were loathe to leave Hemmings and Britten together. These self-righteous old nannies need not have worried, even though the composer was clearly compromising himself. Hemmings was more than master of the situation and having the time of his life:

> '*Of all the people I have worked with, I count my relationship with Ben to have been one of the finest . . . was I aware of his homosexuality? Yes, I was. Was I aware that he had a proclivity for young boys? Yes, I was. Did I find that threatening? No . . .*'

Without such self-knowledge, it is difficult to see how Hemmings could have performed his part so brilliantly, and his absolute loyalty to Britten attests that the trust each had in the other was not misplaced. The danger that Britten must have felt in his relationship with the boy and the queer nature of James's story, feed itself into every scene of the opera, creating a breathless theatrical tension, which, coupled with musical invention of the highest order and its economic use of only six singers and thirteen instrumentalists, makes *The Turn of The Screw* the composer's supreme operatic achievement.

PETER PEARS AND DAVID HEMMINGS
RECORDING BRITTEN'S 'SAINT NICOLAS'
IN ALDBERGH PARISH CHURCH, 1955

BENJAMIN BRITTEN REHEARSING 'NOYES FLUDDE'
IN ORFORD CHURCH, 1958

The tone is blatantly anti-female, pro-male and
especially pro-child, thanks to Britten's own tweaking
of the medieval text and his child-specific casting.

Eternal father

NOYE'S FLUDDE:
LIBRETTO FROM THE CHESTER
MYSTERY PLAYS IN THE
A.W.POLLARD EDITION, FIRST
PERFORMANCE ON 18TH JUNE
1958 IN ORFORD CHURCH

CANTICLE II: ABRAHAM AND
ISAAC: TEXT FROM THE CHESTER
MIRACLE PLAY, FIRST PERFORMANCE
BY KATHLEEN FERRIER, PEARS AND
BRITTEN IN NOTTINGHAM ON 21ST
JANUARY 1952

After playing with fire in *The Turn of The Screw,* Britten's theatrical work focused on the full-length ballet, *The Prince of the Pagodas,* choreographed by Cranko and premièred at Covent Garden on 1st January 1957 with the composer conducting. Meanwhile, Britten was approached by Boris Ford of the London-based commercial television company, Associated Rediffusion, for a new opera, which was to be programmed for schools and based on one of the medieval mystery plays. He had already used A.W. Pollard's edition for *Canticle 2: Abraham and Isaac* and turning to the same source came across the text for *Noye's Fludde.* When the television commission fell through, Britten adopted the idea for production at the Aldeburgh Festival.

Here was a perfect community project that could use dozens of children on stage and in the orchestra, alongside top professional singers and musicians. The story of Noah building the Ark to divine specifications, gathering his family and the animals two by two into the ship to ride out the destruction by flooding of the rest of the world, provided a wonderful, theatrical narrative. It also seemed a safe subject matter after the brave and risky Henry James opera. However, an unfortunate comment by the first conductor, the young Charles Mackerras, about the number of boys in the cast, infuriated the touchy, vulnerable composer. Both boys and girls were needed to play Noah's children and all the animals, to say nothing of recorder players, percussionists mastering the art of slung tea cups, string players and even the buglers of the Boys' Brigade. Britten employed all their varied talents to brilliant dramatic purpose.

He also exploited audience participation, this time in the form of congregational hymns, as he had done previously in *The Little Sweep* and *Saint Nicolas*. Staging the opera in the local church rather than a theatre inspired a liberating use of spatial effects. The animals could be gathered from the four corners of the earth, rushing through the body of the church, while the buglers could be stationed behind the audience, blasting their confident message across time and space. The recording of Colin Graham's original production, made in Orford Church in 1961, captures the spatial vitality so marvellously that original pressings of the vinyl LP (ARGO: ZNF 1) are now prized and valuable collectors' items.

The men in the opera are far more sympathetically treated than the women. God (male), the eternal father, delivers his warning, advice and blessing to Noah alone, ignoring Mrs Noah entirely. She is depicted as ill-tempered, stubborn and ungracious, while her gossips (all female) are a bunch of gibbering idiots who can scarcely see further than the ends of their noses. So tedious are they that we are invited to greet their drowning as a blessed relief. Noah's children and their wives, married adults played by boys and girls, are reasonable and long-suffering, however, as indeed are the ordered and well-behaved animals. It is only Mrs Noah who rocks the boat, endangering all the survivors of the flood. The tone is blatantly anti-female, pro-male and especially pro-child, thanks to Britten's own tweaking of the medieval text and his child-specific casting. Here is a patriarchal world order in which the prime function of all beings female, animal or human, is to procreate. All decision making and practical work is done by males or, as emphasized by Britten, children of either gender.

One cannot ignore the male spite that is generated from God downwards. How cruel of him to destroy the world and most of its creatures because he is dissatisfied with what he, himself, has created. How simple-minded of God to imagine that Noah and his heirs will prove any different from those he has so heartlessly drowned. Yet how easy it is for us to suspend our critical faculties and enjoy this ancient death and resurrection myth, despite its misogynistic undercurrent. Britten's approach endorses the patriarchal order without for one moment challenging its justification. He seems to relish the grotesque caricature of women, embodied in Mrs Noah, making her even nastier in temper than the medieval original. And all this is sanctified unquestioningly by the use of Christian hymns with their grand and moving melodies. Whatever one feels about the substance of the narrative, the emotional impact of this supremely manipulative masterpiece, whether in live performance or recording, drowns all reason. Quite simply, it never fails to bring a gulp to the throat and a tear to the eye, as thousands of productions in schools and colleges, staged in every conceivable venue, have proved over the years.

Britten's earlier excursion into Pollard's edition of medieval mystery plays, the Canticle *Abraham and Isaac,* was written to raise money for the newly formed English Opera Group. The Old Testament story of the father who is ordered by God to slit his son's throat and burn his body in sacrifice is sadistic enough in itself, but, in the context of Britten's operas, a teenage boy threatened with such cruel execution by both his natural and divine fathers has more sinister resonances. The destruction of children by adults is central to *Peter Grimes* and *The Turn of The Screw,* but it is the institutionalized execution of Billy Budd, who is only a year or two older than the teenage Isaac, that springs most abruptly to mind when listening to Britten's concise and intensely dramatic platform piece. In Melville's original story, although the narrator has no direct knowledge of what passed between Captain Vere and the young condemned sailor, he does suggest that Vere 'may in the end have caught Billy to his heart, even as Abraham may have caught young Isaac on the brink of resolutely offering him up in obedience to the exacting behest'. In the Canticle, the ritual exchange of blessings between father and son finds a direct echo in Billy's heroic blessing of Vere before his hanging from the yard arm. Sadly, there is no recording of *Abraham and Isaac* with Ferrier and Pears. However, boy alto John Hahessy (better known today as tenor John Elwes) made an unforgettable recording with Pears and Britten in 1960 (Decca 425 716–2) in which the teenager's terror at his approaching slaughter is deeply disturbing. Unlike the unfortunate Billy Budd, the Eternal Father intervenes at the latest possible moment, thus maximizing the trauma in order to test Abraham's obedience to the limit, and young Isaac lives to see another day.

PETER PEARS AND BENJAMIN BRITTEN IN BERGEN, 1976

Now I have the boy

A MIDSUMMER NIGHT'S DREAM:

LIBRETTO ADAPTED BY BENJAMIN BRITTEN AND PETER PEARS FROM SHAKESPEARE, FIRST PERFORMANCE ON 11TH
JUNE 1960 AT THE JUBILEE HALL, ALDEBURGH

Although discussions were well under way with William Plomer over
what would become the first of the church parable operas, *Curlew River,*
Britten decided to write a full-length opera for the redesigned Jubilee Hall
as part of the 1960 Aldeburgh Festival. By employing an existing text, he
was saving time and eliminating the risk and expense of commissioning a
new libretto. The adaptation that he and Pears produced was primarily a
reduction of the play by half, with only one new line added to a speech of
Lysander for narrative clarification: 'Compelling thee to marry with
Demetrius'. As with the popular and successful *Noye's Fludde,* choosing a
known and much-loved story was also a shrewd commercial decision that
was likely to attract a non-opera-going audience. The Jubilee Hall was
large enough, in its new state, to accommodate a substantial orchestra, so
here was a perfect opportunity to work on a grand scale with a large cast
of principal singers and a chorus of boys. Britten, with characteristic
speed, completed his new opera in a mere seven months.

As Philip Brett points out in his fascinating notes for the Decca CD issue
of Britten's 1966 recording (London 425 663–4), Britten was a master of
camouflaging his own private preoccupations in the public works that he
created. In Shakespeare's play, the squabble between Oberon and Titania
over the Indian changeling boy is embedded in a huge tapestry of
narrative. In the opera, however, Britten and Pears make it the catalyst for
the entire plot. The King of the Fairies and Tytania (Britten's preferred
spelling, officially to revert to supposed Elizabethan pronunciation, but
perhaps to avoid an opera full of Tits?) make their first entry in the middle
of a blazing row over the lad. Oberon wants the 'lovely boy stolen from
an Indian King' so badly that he is prepared to use all his magical powers

to possess him. What, precisely, he wants to do with the 'lovely boy' isn't clear. Oberon already has the adolescent Puck to service his every whim, but the exotic, pre-pubescent child seems to have special attractions. One notes how the composer's own friendships with boys diminished in intimacy once they were well advanced into adolescence. If it weren't for the hallowed name of Shakespeare and for fairies, already sanctioned in classrooms up and down the land, this storyline would strike an audience, rightly, as being thoroughly queer. In 1960, the way Oberon's desire for another boy mirrored Britten's own private preoccupations was known by only a few close friends and colleagues. Today, thanks to Carpenter's biography, that is no longer the case, and our perception of the opera is altered accordingly. Some of Britten's carefully arranged camouflage has thus been stripped away.

All the characters, in Shakespeare's day, would have been played by men and boys, regardless of gender, as would be the case in Britten's church parable operas. But it is strikingly curious that in Oberon's kingdom the only female is Tytania herself. All the fairies are male, even those who are in attendance to the Queen. Oberon has, specifically in Britten's opera, an adolescent boy as his servant. Puck, however, is no piping, pre-pubescent treble but a fully aware, amoral youth, who is given a speaking part in the opera and required by Britten to be a dynamic gymnast, with only mischievous parodies of the mortal lovers to sing with his gutsy, broken voice. Puck shows small interest in the younger fairies, who are only sketchily characterized, with just poor little Moth standing out as he is repeatedly interrupted in mid-flight to charmingly comic effect. It is as though Miles, the boy from *The Turn of The Screw*, has chosen to serve Peter Quint instead of turning to the Governess and so being destroyed. All the magical flights of imagination and enriching experience, promised by Quint in the earlier opera, are found in Oberon and his fairy world, and, at this period of his life, Puck is gloriously happy and free within the limits that his master permits. King Oberon himself has found in Puck the perfect henchman to translate thought into action, give or take an acceptable pinch of boyish wickedness. Here, made flesh, is Quint's longed-for friend:

'OBEDIENT TO FOLLOW WHERE I LEAD,

SLICK AS A JUGGLER'S MATE TO CATCH MY THOUGHT,

PROUD, CURIOUS, AGILE . . .'

Is this the boy that Britten dreamed of but never fully realized in his waking hours?

By starting the opera in the magic wood outside Athens (simply a distant, mythic location for Shakespeare, whose play is otherwise thoroughly English, not Greek), Britten not only leads us straight into a fairy kingdom, but also into the land of night and sleep. Britten had already explored this world in his setting of Keats's sonnet, 'O soft embalmer of the still midnight' in the *Serenade*, Op. 31 (1943), and in the subsequent *Nocturne*, Op. 60 (1958), each written for Peter Pears. The deep-breathing, dreamy, magic kingdom of night is trespassed by two lots of mortals, the lovers and the rustics, each of whom both lose and find themselves in the course of their nocturnal adventures, but are also, as separate social groups, kept apart until the performance of the rustics' play in Act Three. The interweaving of so many storylines with such dramatic purpose and control is just one aspect of Shakespeare's miraculous achievement, an achievement Britten further illuminates with his music.

With so much hilarious and entertaining narrative preserved in the Britten and Pears reduction of the text, it is easy to overlook darker and potentially tragic aspects of the opera. In addition to the sinister desires of Oberon that trigger this anarchic night, violence and disaster are only a sword thrust away from resolving the lovers' disputes and magically induced confusion. Meanwhile, the rustics are in genuine fear of their lives if their play is not approved by Theseus and his guests. Flute warns the other rustics that Bottom's roaring lion: '. . . would fright the Duchess and the Ladies, that they would shriek, and that were enough to hang us all.'

This danger is taken seriously by the amateur thespians, whose brief ensemble: 'That would hang us every mother's son' is superbly coloured by Britten, like a dark cloud across a full moon.

And there is every reason to fear that if Oberon is thwarted in achieving possession of the acutely desired Indian boy, he will abandon playful magic and resort to more violent means. While his 'sweet Queen' is enchanted by his magic, Oberon steals the boy from her care. His satisfaction is confided to 'gentle Robin' (Puck):

'AND NOW I HAVE THE BOY, I WILL UNDO
THIS HATEFUL IMPERFECTION OF HER EYES . . . '

Curiously, Tytania never questions the abduction of the child, nor do we find out what becomes of him, although directors have the opportunity of rounding off this storyline in their productions of both play and opera. Having promoted the importance of the Indian boy in the opera, why didn't Britten and Pears carry this narrative through to a more clear conclusion, at least in the stage directions if not by creating new text? It would have been simple to feature the Indian boy in the stage directions during the anarchic overrunning of Theseus's palace by the fairies at the end of the opera, as indeed, it still can be in production. It would make further sense of the plot if Oberon's possession of the boy was an essential part of his entry and colonization of the palace.

Britten's 1966 recording (London 425 663–2), beautifully conducted and engineered as it is, has curious casting problems. Pears was the original Flute, not Lysander. Playing the rustic, he was, from all reports, hilarious as Thisbe in the play, milking the *bel canto* parody for all it was worth, and having a lot of fun at the expense of Joan Sutherland, who had triumphed recently in *Lucia di Lammermoor* at Covent Garden. Partnered by the ancient sounding Thomas Hemsley as Demetrius, the two male lovers sound absurdly old and unsympathetic. The fairies, like Noah's children in the Argo recording of *Noye's Fludde,* are a posh lot and sound like moonlighters from the local boarding school, as though fairies were the exclusive preserve of the middle classes (mercifully untrue), with Puck (Stephen Terry) as their prep school prefect. Conversely, the Puck on Richard Hickox's recording (Virgin/EMI VCD 59305–2) is the streetwise Londoner Dexter Fletcher, pure urchin and fallen cherub, who rampages through the opera in a way that infuriates Britten traditionalists and delights everyone else. Hickox also restores over a minute of music to Act Three, curiously cut by Britten, even for the Aldeburgh première, at the lovers' awakening.

The social class of the fairies is no trivial matter. The mortals are divided into three clear, ordered, social groupings: rustics, lovers and royalty. If the fairies are pointedly middle class, it makes their final occupation of Theseus's palace simply a capricious act of mischief. In fact, it is the final triumph of anarchy over order, a political act in which all the outsiders (of which Britten's operas are full) invade the establishment and give reign to misrule. The fairies, including Oberon and Tytania, should surely be drawn from all social classes, since the spiteful legislation and prejudices of mere mortals show no class divisions among the outlaws they create.

MYFANWY PIPER

Piper's work on *The Turn of the Screw* had contributed hugely to the creation of one of the greatest twentieth-century operas.

Alive again and straightened out

CURLEW RIVER:	THE BURNING	THE PRODIGAL SON:	OWEN WINGRAVE:
LIBRETTIST WILLIAM	FIERY FURNACE:	LIBRETTIST WILLIAM	LIBRETTIST MYFANWY
PLOMER, FIRST	LIBRETTIST WILLIAM	PLOMER, FIRST	PIPER, PREMIÈRED ON
PERFORMANCE ON	PLOMER, FIRST	PERFORMANCE ON	TELEVISION ON BBC 2
13TH JUNE 1964 IN	PERFORMANCE ON	10TH JUNE 1968 IN	ON 16TH MAY 1971
ORFORD CHURCH	5TH APRIL 1966 IN	ORFORD CHURCH	
	ORFORD CHURCH		

'FROM ALL ILL DREAMS DEFEND OUR EYES,

FROM NIGHTLY FEARS AND FANTASIES;

TREAD UNDERFOOT OUR GHOSTLY FOE

THAT NO POLLUTION WE MAY KNOW.'

(*Te Lucis* . . . . : medieval plainchant)

There was some disquiet in Aldeburgh when the word spread that Peter Pears would be dressing up as a woman to assume a tragic role. Cross-dressing, men as women, and camping it up had long been an acceptable and established British institution, notably in pantomime at Christmas time. Pears himself had cross-dressed to play Thisbe in the rustics' entertainment in *A Midsummer Night's Dream*, but playing a mother, driven mad with grief at the loss of her son, was altogether different. The very idea was challenging and a bit queer, even in the sixties, which may have been swinging in some parts of the world, but not noticeably in polite, dull Suffolk.

The idea for *Curlew River* had been with Britten for at least eight years. He had seen the Japanese Noh play *Sumidagawa* in Tokyo in 1956, with its stylized ritual and all male cast. Having already worked successfully together on *Gloriana,* William Plomer must have seemed the ideal collaborator; he had spent two years in Japan as a young man and had even been offered a Professorial Chair in English Literature in Tokyo at the age of twenty-five, which he declined. His adaptation of the Noh play, transplanting the action to medieval Suffolk and providing a

Christian context for the action, represents his best work as librettist, his slow and deliberate dramatic style harmonizing with the steady unfolding of the Noh narrative.

As usual, the composer had a clear idea of what he wanted and it was Britten who required the singers and musicians to progress through the body of the church, to clothe themselves to assume their characters in the drama, and for the Abbot to address the congregation (i.e. audience) in preparation for the story that follows. Britten had travelled by boat, like the pilgrims in the story, to the island church of San Giorgio Maggiore while staying in Venice, where much of the opera was written, and had witnessed the ritual processing and public robing of the monks, as well as the Abbot's address, all of which were used as the inspirational frame of the new opera.

The Madwoman's twelve-year-old son has been abducted from his family and abused by a cruel man. The search for her boy ends at his grave across the Curlew River, where he is now venerated as a saint. His spirit emerges from the tomb, blesses and then cures her, miraculously, of her insanity. The abuser, who we never see and who, as far as we know, is still at large and repeating his crime elsewhere, is like a distant cousin of Grimes, Black Bob and Quint; all men, who for one reason or another, need boys in their lives and search them out in workhouses, orphanages and, if needs be, from their very homes. One might add Britten to this list, except that, unlike the characters in his operas, although he invited boys into his life to share and enjoy their company, there is no evidence that he was in any way an abusive influence. The dead boy's age is critical, twelve being precisely the age at which young men started to exert their greatest fascination over the composer. There are few periods in life as transitory as puberty. Today's charming cherub is tomorrow's spotty rebel. If Britten's own emotional development seems trapped in eternal adolescence, the reality of actual parenthood, with all its responsibilities, rows and challenges, would surely have shaken his life and household to its foundations.

Once again, Britten was writing for limited resources. The instruments are played by only seven musicians, and, in addition to a small chorus of pilgrims, there are just five singers, including a boy soprano. But as with Britten's other operas using chamber resources, one never feels that economic considerations in any way limit the musical inspiration or dramatic impact. The gradual, stylized pace of the opera, or 'church parable' as Britten preferred to call it, provides an epic and timeless environment for this tale of death and resurrection. Curiously, the single-act drama always seems longer than its sixty-nine minutes (Britten's timing), without ever quite dragging. Its mesmeric quality, focused on the riveting central role of the grief-stricken mother (one of Pears's finest roles in performance and recording: London 421 858–2), and climaxing with the emergence of the dead boy from the grave, is memorable, emotionally harrowing and, especially when performed in an ancient church with its particular ambience and associated history, spiritually cleansing.

Two years after the first church parable opera, *The Burning Fiery Furnace* was premièred, as before, in Orford Church. The format was similar, with monks processing into the church to a medieval hymn (this time *Salus aeterna*) before assuming their duties as performers and musicians. Although vestigial elements of the Noh play tradition remained, the source of the story was the Old Testament rather than another Japanese adaptation. Three Jews are welcomed in Babylon to take up positions of administrative power on account of their 'knowledge and skill'. At a banquet in their honour, boy acolytes provide a cheeky, not to say insulting, entertainment, castigating the Babylonians for their exploitation of natural resources, their dishonesty and their intense greed. Curiously, the courtiers greet this challenging catalogue with cries of 'Good cheer!' The three Jews won't eat the food (surely there was something they could have eaten?) and thus offend their host, Nebuchadnezzar. This misconduct is seized upon by the shifty Chaldean astrologer, who evidently dislikes and mistrusts the foreign influence that has arrived in their midst.

The political subtext that Plomer hammers home is one of racist, xenophobic hostility to immigrants, although, as the Jews have been headhunted at the highest level because of their talents, direct parallels with racism and immigration issues in Britain during the mid-sixties are tenuous. The Jews are, in fact, highly gifted outsiders who dare to challenge the status quo, inspiring similar fears and prejudices as homosexuals in a male-dominated, heterosexual society. But since Babylon is a latter-day Sodom, given, as the boy acolytes graphically point out, to all manner of decadence, attempts to read a profound gay subtext into the story also flounder.

When the Jews refuse to join in the communal worship of Merodak (who?), they are flung into the fiery furnace, which, with the timely assistance of a boy angel who sings a beatific descant, they miraculously survive. Considering the amount of dramatic narrative crammed into a little over an hour, especially when compared to the leisurely *Curlew River,* it is surprising to what degree *The Burning Fiery Furnace* fails to engage the emotions of the 'congregation'. The predicament of the Madwoman in the first opera is truly touching, and her encounter with her son's spirit moves us to tears. It is difficult to care much for the three Jews, who really should have read their job description more carefully, partly because they are scarcely differentiated one from another. We have no opportunity to engage with them as individual characters. Plomer, with his limited dramatic range, seems not to have perceived this problem, let alone attempted to solve it. To make matters worse, Nebuchadnezzar, written specially for Pears, and who might have made a memorable central character, is pure cardboard, as is the wicked astrologer. Only the tireless brilliance of Britten's work with the musicians keeps the show on the road.

The absence of women in Babylon is also a curiosity. The Noh tradition presents no problem in the dramatic representation of women, any more than his all-male companies limited Shakespeare's inspiration. Having tested cross-gender casting in *Curlew River* with notable success, it is odd that Plomer and Britten failed to explore this device further in the church parables, particularly in the third and last of them, *The Prodigal Son.*

Turning this time to the New Testament (and the only true parable of the series), Plomer is on better form, offering a variation on the framing device of the monks' procession by having the Tempter (the Pears part) appear in character from the outset. Only at the end of the opera does he reveal himself as the Abbot. Plomer's text also provides clearly differentiated characters this time. The younger son (the Prodigal), his elder brother and his father each engage us as individuals, while the Tempter himself is like the alter ego of the young prodigal, reminding us also, perhaps because of the distinctive nature of Pears's voice, of Quint and even the newly liberated Albert of 'have a nice peach'.

The Tempter offers the Prodigal only booze, sex and gambling, all of which, the lad should have told him, are readily available in the country. Mischievously, boy sopranos (off stage with words that Britten must have realized would therefore be mostly unintelligible) sing about:

'NIGHTS OF ECSTASY,

JOYS OF FIERCE COMPLETENESS,

BEAUTY OFFERS

PANGS OF PIERCING SWEETNESS.'

The predictability of Plomer's three temptations weaken the plot substantially. The story would have been far more powerful if, for example, in the course of acting out his desires (echoes of Auden), the Prodigal had been compelled for his own survival to steal food from starving children, and commit acts of rape and murder. His selfish actions would thus have had truly sinful consequences, which, in Plomer's libretto, they don't. It might, to advantage, be possible in production for a director to choreograph in what is missing in the text. If the young man is seen to be profoundly sinful, his father's joy and forgiveness on his return home become all the more memorable and cathartic.

It is regrettable that Britten didn't ask Plomer, with his special knowledge of Japanese literature and drama, to find two more Noh plays to adapt, rather than exploit familiar stories from the Bible. One cannot escape the feeling that Britten was working too fast on too many projects, testing his facility for rapid composition to the limits. The biblical church parables, with their formulaic structure borrowed from the innovative *Curlew River*, have too much of the production line about them and suffer accordingly. If there is one common theme shared among the three operas, it is that of death and resurrection. The spirit of the Madwoman's son tells her that:

'THE DEAD SHALL RISE AGAIN
AND IN THAT BLESSED DAY
WE SHALL MEET IN HEAVEN.'

The three Jews survive the fiery furnace, untouched by mortality, and the father of the Prodigal declares to his elder son that:

'. . . THY BROTHER WAS DEAD
AND IS ALIVE AGAIN!'

With cruel irony, it was while Britten was desperately trying to complete *The Prodigal Son* on his usual tight schedule that the heart condition, which would eventually precipitate his own premature death, was diagnosed.

Without mentioning it to Plomer, Britten approached Myfanwy Piper for another adaptation of a Henry James work. Her work on *The Turn of The Screw* had contributed hugely to the creation of one of the greatest twentieth-century operas, and she was the obvious first choice librettist to adapt *Owen Wingrave,* a short story that had been published originally in the *Graphic* magazine in 1892. James had dramatized it himself as a one-act play, but Piper worked from the original story. While her libretto for *The Turn of The Screw* showed filmic influences, with its finely cut short scenes, the new opera was commissioned specially for television and could thus exploit the studio techniques of the period. John Culshaw, who produced many Britten recordings during his time with Decca, had recently become head of music programmes for BBC2. He was responsible for securing Britten's commission for a project that seemed a natural development of the professional relationship he had already established with the composer.

Television drama, even as late as 1970, was mostly studio based and taped using huge, cumbersome cameras, whose versatility was further compromised by the cramped conditions imposed by literal, realistic set design. Its writers and directors generally came to television from a live theatrical background rather than from film-making and the cinema. The use of videotape allowed, among other things, for post-production editing, slow-motion effects, the superimposition of images, crosscutting and, if absolutely necessary, a limited (because of expense) use of film footage. The visual flair of, for example, the young Ken Russell's television films came as a blessed relief from the stagey theatricality and cardboard sets of studio-based drama. Sadly, the production of Britten's new opera would owe more to the latter, musty tradition than the vigorous visual innovations of the former.

Young Owen is being crammed, along with his friend Lechmere, for entry to Sandhurst by Spencer Coyle, with his sympathetic wife providing maternal support to favoured students. Age matters in this drama. Owen and Lechmere are in their late teens, or, at the most, in their early twenties, not middle-aged, late-developing no-hopers. Equally, Kate Julian, with whom Owen has shared his childhood at the family home of Paramore and who is being groomed as the future Mrs Wingrave by her scheming mother, Mrs Julian (another Paramore inmate), is of similar age. While one may suspend one's disbelief over the physical suitability of casting in the opera house, television exposes mercilessly the fact that these characters, scarcely out of childhood, are being played by middle-aged opera singers. Thus Kate, played originally by one of the greatest singers of the century, and no mean actor, Janet Baker, looks far too mature in the original production. The same goes for Benjamin Luxon's Owen, looking not a day under thirty-five. At the other end of the age range, Sylvia Fisher's screaming crow of a Miss Wingrave looks absurdly old to be Peter Pears's daughter. Stated simply, the extraordinary exposure of the television première, which was seen by millions of viewers worldwide, was so marred by miscasting, the theatrical, rather than televisual, acting of artists, and the deadening reek of mothballs pervading the whole presentation, that it has been hard to assess the true merits of the opera ever since. Opportunities of seeing further productions in the theatre have been rare. Its televisual origins present no huge obstacles to theatrical presentation, however, and its relative unpopularity among Britten's operas seems to stem from the dull impression left by its première.

Let's return to basics and see if the story, or more correctly two stories, make any sense. Owen's increasing pacifist convictions lead him to reject a career in the army. As the last of the Wingraves, a family with a dedicated military history, this is too much for his grandfather, General Sir Philip Wingrave, to accept. The old man disinherits Owen, who must also leave the family home of Paramore. The rest of the household are a miserable bunch, evidently devoid of compassion or any sympathetic qualities. One would have thought that Owen would bid them all good riddance with some relief. If Owen looks positively middle-aged, our interest in his predicament is greatly diminished. Conversely, our sympathies are enhanced if he is seen to be a very young man struggling to cope in intolerable circumstances.

Story two concerns the Wingrave ghosts. Generations earlier, a teenage Wingrave refused to fight with his friend and was beaten to death by his furious father. The boy and his murderous father now haunt Paramore, especially, it seems, the murder room. In the opera, Owen agrees to sleep in the haunted room to prove to Kate, who, spiteful bitch, has been flirting openly with Lechmere, that he isn't a coward. Quite unnecessary in the circumstance, one would have thought. For some reason he is found dead. What happened in the haunted room? We don't know. We're not told.

The first story of young Owen's pacifism and his rejection is credible, the second isn't, but we'll go along with it if common sense isn't left high and dry at the end. This is where the relative ages of the characters is important. Owen, in fact, is only a few years older than the murdered boy. He suffers common cause with him. Perhaps his personal sacrifice can lay to rest the boy's wandering spirit. Perhaps the dead boy and Owen share something else in common, a guilty and secret desire, in the case of the murdered boy, for the friend he wouldn't strike, and for Owen, who knows? For the shallow, selfish Lechmere? For Owen's sake, one hopes not. Such a secret passion would appeal both to Henry James (is

'Paramore' a clue?) and Britten, but each was a master at camouflaging private passions. In any event, Myfanwy Piper fails to integrate the two stories convincingly and it is going to be up to the opera's director to paper over the substantial cracks she and Britten have left.

If only she had possessed the dramatic skill to integrate the two stories from the start. Act One is far too long for its content and shows none of the precise focus of her previous work. She falls into the trap of allowing her characters to establish themselves by what they tell us rather than by what they do. Act Two starts with a ballad singer, no character at all in the drama (a poor technical decision), telling us the Wingrave legend of the murdered boy. Then the ghostly dimension is projected into the Owen story. This clumsy structure should have been rejected as the early draft it appears to be. Why couldn't the ghost of the boy have been seen at Coyle's cramming establishment in Act One? Why couldn't Owen and the boy have a scene together? Why don't we see what happens in the haunted room? Why isn't some explanation given for Owen's death? Wonderful dramatic opportunities are missed by Piper, while Britten seems to be content, with his usual facility and imagination, to set the text that is put before him.

One way out of this mess, which won't please Britten purists, is to ignore the existing stage directions, lose the ghost of the boy's father altogether, and introduce just the boy's ghost into Act One. It is vital to the credibility of the plot to establish a kinship between Owen and the dead boy, in their shared attitude to violence, in their true closeness of age, and in their spiritual and emotional need for one another. We simply cannot wait until Act Two to see the ghost. The relationship between Owen and Lechmere, who are both friends and rivals, also mirrors the relationship between the dead boy and the friend (lover?) he would not fight. Anyway, somehow the two stories must be integrated from the outset.

An even more drastic solution would be to take the ballad out of its place at the start of Act Two and, with scissors and paste, introduce some of it into Act One. We do not need to know how the boy met his violent end straight away, and spinning out that narrative could heighten the sense of mystery. The obvious and most simple alternative solution, to transfer the whole of the Wingrave ballad to the start of Act One, probably tells us too much too soon, but is certainly more practical. As for the climax in the haunted room, couldn't the latter part of the scene between Lechmere and the Coyles be played off stage, while what we see is the dead boy drawing the spirit out of Owen in a fatal embrace? This solution would be additionally powerful if the ghost of the dead boy is a late teenager, a precursor of Tadzio perhaps, while Owen is visibly just a few years older, and literally lays to rest the wandering soul of the younger man. Whatever the solution, only an interventionist director can save *Owen Wingrave,* as presently written, from being the ghost of a masterpiece.

PETER PEARS AS ASCHENBACH IN DEATH IN VENICE, 1975

Nothing more natural

DEATH IN VENICE:

LIBRETTIST MYFANWY PIPER, FIRST PERFORMANCE ON 16TH JUNE 1973 IN THE MALTINGS, SNAPE

'Ben is writing an evil opera and it's killing him!' This was a curious off-the-cuff remark for Peter Pears to have made. One might add that for Pears to be on stage for over two hours at the age of sixty-three, acting and singing one of the most demanding roles of his career, might very well have killed him too. Throughout his long relationship with the tenor, Britten had made extraordinary demands on his genius as a performer, including a brutal, psychotic fisherman in *Peter Grimes,* a gay teenager in *Albert Herring,* a gender-bending madwoman in *Curlew River* and now a dying writer in a plague city, obsessed with a Polish boy. But, as Pears acknowledged later, Aschenbach was 'Ben's most wonderful gift to me' and his stage performances, culminating in his now legendary debut at the Metropolitan Opera House, New York, at the age of sixty-four, and the Decca recording conducted by Steuart Bedford, crown an extraordinary career. Pears was truly one of the great actor-singers of the century. The voice may have been odd and distinctive in quality and easy to parody, but his ability to phrase and colour his singing from within the character he was playing was very special. Coupling these qualities with clear articulation, an ability to project a small voice in a large space with absolute clarity, and the skill to convey the rhythms and meanings of words themselves with a poet's ear made him the most original of artists.

That the effort of writing another opera in his poor state of health might indeed have killed the ailing composer is obvious enough, but why did Pears consider it, during its composition, an 'evil opera'? Were old wounds still smarting? Britten's infatuation with David Hemmings at the time of *The Turn of The Screw*'s première in Venice, a sexual passion apparently unconsummated, finds echoes in Thomas Mann's novella both in the obsession of man for boy and in its geographic location. Then there is the

/ay that Britten depended yet again on Pears to be the public and performing face of his own private and secret passion for boys. Then there was also the 'evil' of the stress that attempting to write such an ambitious opera introduced into Britten's exhausting schedule, to say nothing of the additional problem, both artistic and legal, of the Visconti film, which was being made while Britten and Myfanwy Piper were working on the opera. Britten, under advice, made a point of not seeing the film, partly in case he should be accused of borrowing ideas from it. Where film and opera differ most markedly is in their respective treatments of the boy Tadzio. Visconti's Tadzio is a pretty, blond tart who flashes his eyes and arse at the besotted Aschenbach, superbly played by Dirk Bogarde, shamelessly. Britten's Tadzio, by contrast, is represented by a dancer with both Apollonian and Dionysian qualities, a meeting point of reason and sensuality, and an altogether more complex characterization which lifts the entire opera onto a different artistic and philosophical level.

Britten's choice of Myfanwy Piper as librettist was logical enough, even if doubts over her technical facility had managed to penetrate the tight inner circle of the composer's household after *Owen Wingrave*. He liked and trusted her and should, by then, have been aware of her strengths and shortcomings. In the event, her libretto for *Death In Venice* is mostly excellent. What she conspicuously lacks is any streetwise sense, so that the youths and the elderly fop and the boatloads of boys and girls in Act One sound laughably polite and upper-crust English, especially in the Decca recording (London 425 669–2), which is more like Death in Henley than Venice. Her original libretto also included the line 'All my art is bent', which the more worldly Pears suggested was a little unfortunate. Such an obvious gaffe tells us much about the protected environment in which Britten, who also, presumably, saw nothing wrong with the line, and Piper lived.

A number of crucial artistic decisions dictated the structure of the libretto. Aschenbach's story is told in chronological order. No time shifts. No framing devices. The principal characters that he encounters, Traveller, Gondolier, Hotel Manager and Barber, and the Leader of the Players are played by one singer, originally the brilliant John Shirley-Quirk, who, additionally, is also the voice of Dionysus in the dream sequence of Act Two. This presents Piper with the significant challenge of creating enough time for both Aschenbach and the multi-role singer to get on and off stage between the continuously linked scenes and, as necessary, to get changed from one character to another and move from one location to another. Opera librettists have one helpful card always up their sleeves, the orchestral interlude, with which the composer can dig them out of trouble. To her great credit, Piper manages the technical mechanics of the opera's complicated narrative structure with ease, and brief orchestral passages exist for purely artistic reasons and not to assist the librettist's development of the plot. Especially noteworthy is the way the different narrative moments are dovetailed into each other with increasing rapidity as the story reaches its conclusion in Act Two. Thus, in Scene Nine: 'The Pursuit', we follow Aschenbach crossing to Venice in a gondola, witnessing the citizens reading notices about health precautions, encountering shopkeepers and various street characters, making decisions about whether to tell the Polish family about the epidemic, seeing Tadzio and his family in a café, following them to St Mark's, participating in the service and then coming face to face with the family and finding himself unable to say anything to them at all, and so on. All this is accomplished in a single sequence with the utmost economy and skill of a great storyteller. It shows Piper returning to her cinematographic style of *The Turn Of The Screw* to valuable effect.

Britten and Piper also introduce the god Apollo, sung by a counter-tenor, into the narrative. He presides over extended games, a pentathlon, for Tadzio and the boys in which Tadzio is the victor. Contained therein is a Greek ideal of masculine intelligence and beauty expressed in athletic achievement, which in Victorian and Edwardian England was part of the ethos of the British public school. The homoerotic, Dionysian character of such narcissistic display was officially seen as something dangerous and morally corrupting in those august institutions, however much the homoerotic element was unofficially enjoyed by boys and staff alike. And so it is with Aschenbach, whose initial worship of Tadzio's divine beauty tries hard to be aesthetic as opposed to lustful. Visconti's too knowing Tadzio fails miserably, if beguilingly, to convey this crucial dimension in Mann's story. In the opera, Aschenbach's struggle to reconcile the Apollonian and Dionysian aspects of his passion constitute the heart and soul of the drama. In an explicitly sexual dream sequence, Aschenbach witnesses a confrontation between Apollo and Dionysus (Scene Thirteen), culminating in a graphic musical orgasm as Tadzio himself appears. What a contrast between the explosive rapture of this music, which impacts on our senses like the 'Once in a while . . .' from *Paul Bunyan* all those years ago, and the brutal abuse of Lucretia by Tarquinius, where, as previously suggested, no male orgasm is, in fact, achieved in Britten's music by the rapist.

After the orgasmic liberation of the dream, and Aschenbach's acceptance that surrendering to his pederastic instinct is less destructive than trying to sublimate it in an unrealized, passionless aestheticism, he finds himself becoming almost indistinguishable from the Elderly Fop that so disgusted him on his arrival in Venice. Aschenbach's decision to eat fresh and almost certainly contaminated strawberries when he knows that the Polish family are leaving and he now has no chance of transforming his infatuation for Tadzio into physical reality, is almost like fulfilling a death wish, like a latter-day Tristan, and like another pederastic composer, Tchaikovsky, who, at the time Britten was writing his opera, was wrongly thought to have contracted cholera by deliberately drinking contaminated water.

Aschenbach's tragedy is that, like Britten, like Thomas Mann, like Henry James, he was too scared, too fearful of rejection, too morally confused, or too emotionally damaged, to explore the Dionysian side of his personality. The distinction between the paedophile and the pederast is the difference between the piping treble of Miles, the pubescent boy, and the muscular, inquisitive young manhood of the dancer Tadzio or the tumbling Puck. For Aschenbach or Britten to admit as each faces death that a huge and important part of their lives has been stunted by repressive laws and emasculated by stale, hypocritical morality, can lead only to horror and despair.

Against medical advice, Britten postponed a heart operation so that he could complete the opera. Unfortunately, during the eventual operation, it is suspected that a small piece of calcium was carried to his brain through his bloodstream and lodged there. This effected the coordination of his right hand and left him partially incapacitated. He survived in increasing ill-health for a further three years. Britten died peacefully in the arms of his partner in December 1976. Peter Pears outlived him by ten years. They lie buried next to each other in Aldeburgh parish churchyard.

PETER PEARS AND BENJAMIN BRITTEN
AT SNAPE, SUFFOLK, 1974

Picture credits

Absolute Press would like to thank Pam Wheeler at The Britten-Pears Library for all her help in the production of this book.

Pg. 6	© Christopher Wilson. Courtesy of Mrs Joan Plant
Pg. 11	Courtesy of Britten Pears Library
Pg. 18	© Bridget Kitley. Photograph by Enid Slater
Pg. 30	© Cyril Arnold (untraced in 1997)
Pg. 38	© Cyril Arnold (untraced in 1997)
Pg. 50	© Peter Hutton. Photograph by Kurt Hutton
Pg. 58	© holder unidentified 1997. Courtesy of Britten-Pears Library
Pg. 64	© Peter Hutton. Photograph by Kurt Hutton
Pg. 69	© Peter Hutton. Photograph by Kurt Hutton
Pg. 70	© Peter Hutton. Photograph by Kurt Hutton
Pg. 74	© Hans Rowe
Pg. 80	© John Harris
Pg. 90	© Nigel Luckhurst
Pg. 94	© Victor Parker
Pg. 96	Courtesy of the Britten Pears Library

BRITTEN AND PEARS WITH PRINCESS MARGARET AND PRINCE LUDWIG OF HESSE AND THE RHINE IN VENICE 1956